FINANCIAL TIPS FOR THE FAMILY

Financial Tips for the Family

Keith Tondeur

Hodder & Stoughton
LONDON SYDNEY AUCKLAND

Copyright © Keith Tondeur 1997

First published in Great Britain 1997

The right of Keith Tondeur to be identified as the Author of the Work has been asserted by him in accordance with the Copyright, Designs and Patents Act 1988.

10 9 8 7 6 5 4 3 2 1

British Library Cataloguing in Publication Data
A record for this book is available from the British Library

ISBN 0 340 68673 1

Printed and bound in Great Britain by
Cox & Wyman Ltd, Reading, Berks

Hodder and Stoughton Ltd
A Division of Hodder Headline PLC
338 Euston Road
London NW1 3BH

CONTENTS

Acknowledgments vii

Introduction 1

1 The background 3
 The world of money: a dangerous place

2 Communication 9
 Talking to your partner – and listening

3 Budgeting 15
 Why and how: making an estimated monthly
 budget – and balancing it
 Working out your assets and liabilities

4 Standard of living 27
 Deciding what's best: how to set your goals

5 Housing and cars 33
 Houses: how to choose and how to pay
 Cars: thinking twice and saving money

6 Using credit 51
 Credit – or debt? Different ways of borrowing: the
 pros and cons

7 Debt 61
 Taking action and getting help; credit reference
 agencies; dealing with creditors

Contents

8 Giving   69
Increasing the value of what you give: covenants,
payroll giving, Gift Aid, inheritance tax

9 Savings   73
Banks, building societies, National Savings,
TESSAs, PEPs, bonds, pensions

10 Insurance   81
For cars, house contents, buildings, health and
loan protection

11 Taxation   95
Indirect and direct taxation: VAT, Council Tax,
income tax, National Insurance
How taxes are assessed and collected; self
assessment, capital gains, inheritance tax
Tax-saving hints

12 Your children and money   113
Suggestions for teaching financial skills; dealing
with peer pressure; funding college

13 Saving on food   123
Planning a money-saving menu; shopping; ideas
for good cheap meals

14 And what about . . . ?   137
Work, redundancy, time management, benefits
Where to go for advice

15 Conclusion   147

Address list   149

ACKNOWLEDGMENTS

I am very grateful to a number of people who have contributed towards this book. My thanks go to Rob Parsons and Jonathan Booth for their help and support in the preparation. Particular thanks to Michael Wilson and Gordon Pickering who did almost all the work on insurance, savings and tax. Thanks also to Kate Pickering for her help with the typing.

INTRODUCTION

Managing money within the family has never been more difficult. The constant pressures tell us that we 'need' so many things and that it is vital to 'keep up with the Joneses', wear the latest fashions and keep the children quiet by buying them the latest expensive toy. In fact, we are encouraged to spend, spend, spend. We live in an instant gratification society where our credit cards and the 'buy now, pay nothing for six months' mentality encourages us to think we can afford payments that in reality we cannot. Why bother saving when spending money is such fun?!

But there is a reverse side to this, and it is seen in the appalling number of debt problems in this country and the millions of people currently on credit 'blacklists'. Hardly anyone has been taught by their parents or in school how to handle money sensibly, yet we spend hours every day earning, spending, giving and saving money and increasingly worrying about it.

The aim of this book is to stretch your money further. If you're in debt you could be wasting hundreds of pounds a month in paying interest; if just about in balance, there may well be ways of unlocking significant amounts for saving; and if you are saving it should help ensure that you are maximising your return. In addition, handling money within the family can cause enormous tension and is named by many as the major cause of marriage breakdown. So within the book there are sections on communication as well as on how to teach your children to handle money sensibly.

By following the advice in various sections of this book you should be able to create an environment which will enable you to discuss and plan your future financial goals so that everyone in your family will benefit.

1
THE BACKGROUND

The way we spend money today should probably carry a government health warning! Many of us do not seem to realise that credit makes assumptions about tomorrow and that if we suddenly suffer a major reverse we will not be in a position to do much about it. In addition, the people who only recently have been encouraging you to part with your money or borrow even more tend to change the tone of their letters quite dramatically when you are struggling to maintain payments.

Budgeting and avoiding over-commitment is not just about saving money – although that is very important. It is also about the removal of stress and improving your health, your self-esteem and your marriage. As the following figures indicate, millions of people in this country have fallen victim to debt-related problems:

- In the last five years approximately 700,000 people have lost their homes as 300,000 properties have been repossessed.

- Over 3 million court summonses are issued for debt each year.

- At any one time there are more people in prison for unpaid fines than for any other reason.

Nearly all of these cases will not only involve financial hardship but will include marital tension and often loss of self-worth. Sadly, we live in a society that tends to judge people by material success ('Hello, how are you? And what do you do?'). So when redundancy or a lower standard of living strikes we can so easily be made to feel like failures. Living on benefits only adds to this kind of pressure. So for some it is the basic lack of things that causes heartache, while for others it is the loss of them. But both categories find it difficult to talk about their money problems. Frequently it is easier simply to pretend that the situation doesn't exist and hope that it will go away than face up to it. So often the problem is just left and debts steadily accumulate. But only good can come out of seeking sensible advice from independent experts. So whatever your financial position, never be afraid to seek out those who can help.

If you are sitting there thinking that this does not really apply to you then I have to tell you that a recent article stated that the average British family is only weeks away from bankruptcy. It went on to say, 'The average family has little or no money saved, a large amount of fixed monthly living expenses, an increasing amount of credit commitments and total dependence on next month's income just to keep going.'

Just imagine for a moment that next month's pay cheque doesn't arrive or that your Giro is late. That in itself can make us feel very worried. And this applies right across our society today because, generally speaking, the more people earn the more they borrow. So there are 'rich' people with very well-paid jobs whose finances would be devastated by illness, accident or redundancy.

The problem is clear. Far too few of us know enough about our own finances. It may well be that we don't want to know because if we worked out the total amount of our liabilities we would be very worried. Lack of knowledge about our situation is a very clear indicator that we aren't in control of our finances. So right at the beginning of this book let me ask you some basic questions:

- Do you know reasonably accurately how much your fixed living expenses are (i.e. mortgage payments or rent, food, gas, electricity, water, Council Tax, phone, TV licence, insurance, etc.)?

- Do you know, without looking it up, the total of your outstanding debts (i.e. credit and store cards, hire purchase agreements, bank loans and overdrafts, etc.)?

- Are you aware of the current rates of interest being charged on your debts if you don't pay them on time? This is particularly important when it comes to credit and store card balances because if the full amount is not paid off every month (and this is true in the majority of cases) then interest is charged on all of the outstanding debt.

Then you need to ask yourself the following questions which will help show if you have your finances under control:

- Do you regularly spend impulsively using store or credit cards?

- Have you taken out any new credit commitments in the last twelve months?

- Do you regularly miss paying off your credit card payments on time?

- Do you find it impossible to save money regularly?

- Do you ever withhold financial information from your partner?

- Have you ever bought lottery tickets or scratch cards

because winning seems to be the only way to resolve your problems?

If you answered 'yes' to any of these questions, please don't feel guilty or hopeless and certainly don't stop reading! Managing money is very difficult and seems to be getting harder. There are several reasons for this:

- **Personal debt** The amount of personal debt has more than trebled in real terms over the last fifteen years and now stands well in excess of £60 billion – and this figure excludes mortgages. With around 45 million credit and store cards in circulation this trend is likely to continue.

- **Government debt** Over the last few years there has been a sharp increase in the National Debt. This has led to government policies aimed at cutting state spending where at all possible. Some of these measures, such as the extension of the period before Income Support pays mortgage interest for the unemployed, for example, increase the burden on the individual.

- **Consumerism/materialism** We live in a society where 'having' increasingly seems more important than 'being'. Advertising tells us that we 'need' so many things – and that somehow our family is not complete unless we have them. In addition all too easily available credit and all the 'buy now and pay nothing till later' schemes mean we can be sucked into over-commitment before we realise what is happening.

- **Peer pressure** The pressure that society puts on us adults to appear successful and fit in is enormous. At school and especially as teenagers our children can face it even more, and may even be bullied if they don't wear the right designer labels or trainers.

The Background

Given all these pressures, it is easy to see how so many families struggle with money. But having listed them it is now important to move on and start taking action to improve the situation.

2
COMMUNICATION

Before we even begin to move on to some practical issues it is important that the issue of communication in the family is addressed – and particularly that between husband and wife. A key step in solving the various problems that money can cause in a marriage is a plan to communicate. This needs to be not just about specific money issues but also your priorities as a couple. For example, to say, 'Darling, I just wanted to let you know that I'm going to bet all my month's salary on the Grand National,' is clearly a communication, but it is unlikely to provoke a harmonious reaction!

Communication is vital. Although problems may seem to be about money, in some cases they are more to do with communication, or the lack of it. There are many times when I have been counselling a couple and the wife has said to me, 'If he would only talk to me and let me know what is going on, things would be much better.' Equally her husband may say, 'She doesn't understand just how hard I'm working at this current time and yet all she seems to do is keep on spending.' It is also important to recognise that when husbands and wives do talk to each other, although they both use English they are often speaking in different languages! This was brought home to me fairly recently when my wife asked me to take the rubbish out and I said 'yes'. What we actually meant was the following:

Carole (my wife): Please take the rubbish out (NOW!).

9

Keith: Yes, I will take the rubbish out (some time before the year 2010!).

It really is so easy to misunderstand each other and because the issue of money is particularly volatile it is so easy for a discussion to rapidly develop into an argument, which can then make us resentful or afraid of bringing up the subject again. If you value your relationship highly you will endeavour to do whatever is necessary to talk to your partner and not allow your money problems to disrupt it. In order to help I have listed some guidelines below.

The first thing you need to understand is how your partner reacts to different and difficult circumstances. Each of us reacts when we are upset about things, but it can be in very different ways. Some people become very silent, some bring out other things they are annoyed about, while others may try and pretend there's nothing wrong by busying themselves with things like the ironing. As soon as these reactions have been understood they must be faced. It is important to be sensitive but if they are ignored an even bigger frustration will develop. The best way, I believe, to respond in such a situation is to ask a question like, 'Is anything bothering you?' This shows that you have picked up on something, that you care about your partner's feelings and want to respond to them.

Second, if you are upset and your partner has not picked it up then it is your responsibility to say something. The earlier you do this the better it will be.

Once the problem has been brought out into the open and there is agreement that a problem needs to be resolved you can start to talk about it. In many cases it is easy for one partner to ask, 'Is anything wrong?' and the other to reply 'No' when obviously the answer is 'Yes'. 'No' is almost always the normal reaction every time. It takes perception, consistency and sensitivity to draw out the root of the problem.

When you are talking there are other guidelines you need

to observe, even though they are often difficult to do! So try not to shout, don't be antagonistic and don't ever make insulting or derogatory remarks. Often when talking to my wife I feel like saying something like, 'That's a stupid thing to say!' This kind of remark will only disrupt the harmony and break down lines of communication even more. Stay calm and talk through the problem. When conflicts are worked through and resolved they become stepping stones to a stronger marriage – but the longer they are allowed to fester the more danger is caused to the relationship.

As you discuss the problem try to agree on some specific steps that will help solve it. In the area of finances, for example, a specific step that will provoke harmony is to produce a family budget and, with the input and agreement of both partners, assign specific areas of responsibility.

One of the main reasons for the need for good on-going communication is the emotional pressure that money can bring with it. Debt, the loss of overtime or the fear of redundancy can create the most enormous problems for people. One of the saddest things is that when the unexpected does happen to us financially, very few know what to do next. This is usually because we have never been taught how to handle money in the first place, let alone when things start to go wrong. That is why most of us not only fail to budget but often live up to or even slightly beyond our credit limits. It is therefore no wonder that panic sets in when income suddenly threatens to dry up.

It is this talk of education that often gets us into trouble in the first place. It is so easy to spend impulsively, significantly underestimate our essential out-goings and at the same time not make allowances for sudden adverse events like major house repairs or a belated tax bill. Equally, most financial agreements are difficult to understand. We don't bother with the small print because we haven't understood the large! Many of us end up signing things we understand very little about.

It is important to know that money troubles rarely strike

in isolation. They are often tied in with more pressures as well as relationship problems. In fact in a survey of couples who split up, money was named by over 70 per cent as the number one cause of the problem. For example, if your partner leaves unexpectedly it will be immensely emotionally draining and what little energy you have left will probably be used up looking after your children and ensuring that they are coping as best they can. The bills that are steadily accumulating on the mantelpiece will not seem that important to you just now, but debt is creeping up on you even though you are too emotionally tense at this time to do anything about it.

Whenever we take out credit we are making assumptions that we will be able to repay it out of future income that has not yet been received – and it may be that it will not come our way! We can borrow for all sorts of reasons – we are poorly paid, receive insufficient benefit, have been 'persuaded' by advertising that we 'need' various new products or have simply succumbed to our own personal desires to have more. When things go wrong, therefore, a whole range of emotions can burst to the surface, including fear, anger and guilt. It is vitally important at this stage that you are totally open with your partner about your financial worries. Because of the pressures you are facing, and particularly if you are afraid that your partner will be upset, worried or angry because of the financial situation, it is very tempting to say nothing and just hope that things will work out. But by doing this you are almost certainly only storing up future trouble for yourself. Your partner cannot help resolve the situation – by changing spending habits, for example – if they are unaware there is a problem in the first place. Equally, when they do find out after a period of time it will not be the money worries that will be uppermost. Rather it will be the lack of trust – the 'Why did you think you couldn't tell me?' syndrome. As this can so easily be coupled with the thought 'I wonder what else I haven't been told?' it becomes very clear that relationships can be put under real strain at these times.

Despite the fact that millions of people can suffer money problems through no fault of their own, it remains a stigma and the emotional pressures can lead to rational people doing very irrational things. If you are facing these emotional issues, recognise first that you are not alone and that it is no way a reflection on you as being some sort of 'failure'. Recognise too that you will need help. The chapter on debt should be useful here. Regardless of your current financial situation you need to be talking to your partner and agreeing the best way forward for your family.

3
BUDGETING

The only certain way of demonstrating some financial control is to learn how to budget. This is not just for people who are in debt or are struggling to make ends meet. It will help everyone make their money go further. Often people are not willing to begin to budget because they are afraid of what will be revealed when they do! We don't really know where our money goes because we don't look, and we don't look because we don't really want to know!

If you are not budgeting then at best you are handling your money by 'guesstimates' and at worst you are just hoping things will work out all right. Living by a budget will undoubtedly make your money go further and this will be especially useful to those who recognise that often there is 'too much month left at the end of the money'. A budget will help you guide and prioritise your spending. It should also make it much, much easier to stay in financial control. It will also show you where your money is actually going. Often our perceptions of priorities – children's clothing or heating, for example – are destroyed when we see just how much we are spending on video rentals, trips to the pub and meals out!

What is a budget? A budget is simply your family's plan for spending money.

WHY BUDGET?

As you may by now have realised, budgeting is not one of the most exciting things in the world to do, but it is one of the most important. It is the only way to follow through and apply what has been learned about getting out of debt, saving and giving while still meeting your basic needs. It may seem remarkable but, regardless of income, most of us will be struggling to make ends meet unless there is a plan for spending. Expenses always seem to manage to rise that little bit faster than income.

But budgeting is not just practically important: there are emotional ramifications as well. In the majority of families with financial problems there are emotional pressures and real tension. In fact, money worries are almost certainly the major cause of marital break-up. To be successful, a budget has to be a team effort with both partners actively involved. A budget should aim to ensure that a family gets full value for its money without losing sight of individual priorities and preferences.

HOW TO BUDGET

A budget is no use if it is done and then hidden away in a drawer. It needs to be used. And it should be a plan that is tailor-made for managing your family's finances, not any-one else's. Some people are more comfortable working on a hand-written system while others will prefer using a ready-prepared budget system on a computer. To set up your family budget you need to follow these three steps:

Begin where you are today
As you develop your budget you must start with the reality of your current situation, and therefore you need to determine precisely how much money is earned and spent. This may sound straightforward but sadly most people are unaware of what they are actually earning and spending. For this reason it is essential to keep a detailed record of everything you spend during a period of at least a month in order to complete an accurate estimate of your budget. The easiest way of doing this is for every spending member of the family to have a pocket-sized notebook and write in it absolutely everything they spend. Remember, this is not being done in

order to criticise each other's spending habits but simply to gain an accurate picture of your family's spending.

It is important that you have an accurate assessment of your income as well. If you are self-employed or a salesperson whose income is heavily commission-orientated it is just as important to do this. What you need to do is make a conservative estimate of your annual income and divide by twelve to establish a working figure for your monthly income.

You then also need to work out expenses that do not necessarily occur every month, such as insurance and holidays. Estimate how much you spend on these each year and then divide by twelve to determine your monthly cost. Once you have gathered all this information together you can complete the estimated monthly budget that follows. Whatever you do, do not get discouraged at this stage. Almost every budget starts with expenditure in excess of income, but solutions do exist!

Estimated monthly budget
YOUR PERSONAL BUDGET:
DETAILS OF MONTHLY INCOME

Your basic salary	£
Spouse's basic salary	£
Guaranteed overtime	£
(Flexible overtime)*	£
(Flexible bonuses)*	£
Pension	£
Child Benefit	£
Income Support	£
Family Credit	£
Other benefits	£
Maintenance	£
Disability benefits	£

TOTAL INCOME   £

* Put in brackets but do not add to total as these figures cannot be relied on week after week. When they occur use to pay off debts or save, as appropriate.

YOUR PERSONAL BUDGET:
DETAILS OF MONTHLY EXPENDITURE
Formal commitments

Mortgage	£	TV licence	£
Rent	£	Car MOT	£
Water rates	£	Road tax	£
Ground rent	£	Vehicle insurance	£
Service charge	£	Regular giving	£
Council Tax	£	Personal insurance	£
Property insurance	£	Private pension	£
Home contents insurance	£	Maintenance payments	£
Electricity	£	Second mortgage	£
Gas	£	Loan repayments	£
Oil	£	HP repayments	£
Coal	£	Credit card payments	£
Telephone	£	School fees	£
	£	Other	£

Formal commitments – Total 1   £

Everyday spending

Food and sundries	£	TV rental	£
Children's pocket money	£	Video rental	£
Childminder	£	Evening classes	£
Toys and books	£	Tapes and CDs	£
Pet food	£	Alcohol	£
Laundry/dry cleaning	£	Cigarettes	£
Chemist	£	Newspapers, magazines	£
Parking	£	Petrol	£
Public transport	£	Other	£

Everyday spending – Total 2   £

Occasional costs

Christmas	£	Vet bills	£
Birthdays	£	Clothing	£
Holidays	£	Dentist	£
Car repairs	£	Optician	£
House repairs	£	Trips, outings	£
Redecoration	£	Meals out	£
Replacement furniture	£	Other	£

Occasional costs – Total 3   £

TOTAL MONTHLY EXPENDITURE

Total 1	£
Total 2	£
Total 3	£

GRAND TOTAL   £

BALANCE

Monthly income	£
Monthly expenditure	£
Monthly surplus/deficit	£

Move to where you want to be

To solve the problem of spending more than you earn you need either to increase your income or to decrease your spending. It really is that simple. Earn more or spend less. There really are no other alternatives.

How can you add to your income? Another part-time job or, better still, a project that could involve the whole family are ways of increasing your income. Remember, though, that there is always a danger that expenses tend to rise when extra jobs are taken on. To avoid this problem you need to agree from the beginning that all the extra income generated will be used in helping balance the budget. It is vital, if you are thinking of going down this route, to consider the potential negative impact it would have on your family. Relationships matter immensely and you need to be thinking about the signals you are sending to your children if you are working long hours every day to continue a certain lifestyle, but have little or no time to be with the people you love.

If increasing income is not the answer, then reducing expenses is the only way. The first thing to do, as a family, is to look at your expenses and ask yourselves the following questions:

- Which are absolutely necessary?

- Which can we do without?

- Which can we substantially reduce?

Again, do not spend all your time telling other members they need to cut back. Start with yourself!

Here are some guidelines to help you evaluate your major expenses. Actual figures will very much depend upon the cost of housing where you live and the size and age of your family. But if you are substantially above any of these figures they probably indicate an area you should begin to evaluate very carefully.

Percentage guideline

Category	% of income after tax
Housing	30
Utilities/Council Tax, etc.	10
Food	12
Transport	15
Insurance	3
Entertainment/recreation	5
Clothing	5
Giving/saving (or, initially, debt repayments)	15
Miscellaneous	5

There is a whole variety of ways in which a family can cut back on its expenditure. I have listed below just a few main ideas in some of the major categories, but to examine how this can be done in more detail please study chapter 13, which looks at a whole range of ways you can reduce your spending on food. Obviously, these suggestions do not apply to everyone. Equally, you may well have many good ideas of your own. With a little imagination these ideas could expand to form another book on their own! But let me mention just a few under various headings.

Housing
- If you have do-it-yourself skills be prepared to buy an older house that you can improve by working on it yourself in your own time.

- Remember, the smaller the house the lower the cost of the utilities will usually be.

- Lower the cost of utilities by limiting the use of heating, lighting and appliances.

- Shop carefully for furniture and appliances. Take full advantage by buying direct or by buying in genuine sales.

- When buying a home always have a proper survey done. This will highlight problems that need to be faced, and you should be able to deduct the cost of this from your purchase.

Transport
- Do whatever you can to use only one car.

- Remember that as soon as you drive a new car off the garage forecourt its value has depreciated considerably, so buy a lower-cost used car and keep it until the repair bills start becoming too expensive.

- Usually smaller cars are more economical to run.

- Try and perform routine maintenance yourself – things such as changing the oil. This will not only work out quite cheaply but should also prolong the life of your car.

Clothing
- Plan your spending in advance. Make a written list of your family's yearly clothing needs. Shop from this list during the off-season sales.

- Try and purchase simple basic fashions that you can add to, rather than follow fads which will change so quickly.

- Do not over-purchase. Select two or three basic colours and then buy outfits you can wear in combination with others.

- Clothes that can be washed at home are much cheaper to maintain than those that need to be commercially cleaned.

Insurance
- Shop around and make sure you only get cover for what your family really needs.

- Sometimes raising the initial sum you are prepared to pay yourself will substantially reduce your premiums.

- Ask your friends for recommendations.

Entertainment and recreation
- Draw up a list of things that the family can do in the vicinity that are either very cheap or completely free.

- Stick to a limit, including spending money, on holidays and then book somewhere accordingly.

Budgeting

As well as the above, here are five hints to help you with budgeting:

1 Reconcile your cheque book monthly. It is so easy for mistakes to occur or even for relatively large cheques to empty your bank account. Failure to take account of them can have serious consequences.

2 It can be sensible to open up a separate savings account where every month you can deposit the required monthly allowance for the bills that do not fall due on a regular monthly basis. For example, if you had an annual insurance premium of £360 you would deposit £30 in this savings account each month. Doing this ensures that there is enough money available to pay this type of bill when it becomes due.

3 Occasionally, rather than thinking weekly or monthly, think yearly! This can sometimes really bring home the annual cost of something. For example, if you spend £4 on lunch each working day your annual lunch bill will be very near £1,000. Thinking yearly shows the true cost of apparently inconsequential day-to-day expenses.

4 Be so aware of impulse spending. This can range from buying expensive one-off items like cars or holidays to smaller items like fashions, chocolates or magazines. Impulse spending is the big budget buster. I suggest that every time you have the urge to buy something you have not planned for, you put it on a list and keep this list at home for at least a week. See if it is still so much of a 'need' at the end of this time! At the same time use this period to see if this bargain you have spotted is really as good value as it seems. Is it the best model? Can it be bought more cheaply elsewhere? What exactly do you need it for? Of course, at the end of the week it is still possible to make the purchase

23

if it is right for your family, but many people rush in and buy impulsively, burst their budget and repent at leisure.

5 Remember that both husbands and wives should have some personal allowances in the budget to spend as they please. Should I decide to squander money, therefore, by going to watch Lincoln City try to play football, then that is entirely down to me as long as the allowance holds out. This should help eliminate many arguments.

The next step is vital:

Do not stop!
Whatever you do – keep at it. Remember, a budget is simply a plan for spending your family's income. It will not work by itself. Every area of your budget needs to be reviewed regularly in order to keep spending money in check. From time to time you will undoubtedly face frustrations, but if properly used a budget will save you literally thousands of pounds. It will not only help you stay out of debt but it should also allow you to accumulate savings. Even more important, it will help provide a basic form of communication for husband and wife in the area that is a leading cause of marital tension and conflict.

ASSETS AND LIABILITIES STATEMENT

At the same time as drawing up your budget it makes sense to produce your family's assets and liabilities statement. You do not have to be absolutely precise at this stage, just estimate the amount of each asset and liability as accurately as you can. Then you need to look at the list and see if there are any assets that you no longer require and could sell or liabilities that you could reduce. One way of doing this could be to move to a smaller house. What action you take really does depend on your overall financial position at the time. Have a look at the assets and liabilities statement shown here and produce your own.

Assets and liabilities statement
(Estimate as accurately as possible)

ASSETS (present market value)   **£**

Home
Car/motorbike
Caravan
Computer
Furniture
Consumer goods
Cash
Savings
Shares
Cash value of life insurance
Stamps/coins
Jewellery
Pension plan
Other assets

LIABILITIES (current amount owed)   **£**

Mortgage
Credit arrangements
Credit cards
Store cards
Overdrafts
Loans
Personal debts
Utility debts
Tax/National Insurance
Other 'secured' loans
Other 'unsecured' loans

NET WORTH (total assets less total liabilities)   **£**

By reviewing your assets and liabilities statement regularly, and I suggest you do it as a family at least yearly, you will get a very good picture of what trends are taking place and also – I hope – see an encouraging growth of your family's net worth.

4

STANDARD OF LIVING

One of the first things you need to do as a family is to ascertain your standard of living. To some this may seem a rather ridiculous thing to discuss – surely everyone wants theirs to be as high as possible? But it really isn't as simple as that. If, for example, you have several children, all of whom may be going to college in a few years' time, then it may well be more prudent to accept a lower standard of living now in order that they may be helped in their student years – particularly now that government grants have been cut so much.

Questions about standards of living are always important because they involve raising some pretty major points. Should the family move to a larger house, or stay in the present one and try and clear the mortgage as soon as possible? Should we purchase a bigger car, and if so should it be a new one? Should the family adopt a more expensive lifestyle or continue to save and give more?

When we are thinking about what is best for our family we often should be focusing on the longer term. This can be quite difficult when our culture and the media tell us to focus on the immediate. Advertisers are constantly telling us that as consumers we should happily gratify ourselves today with no thought of tomorrow. But to follow this route exposes us to enormous risks – particularly if we use credit to finance our standard of living. As millions of people have eventually found out to their cost, there are no longer many, if any, guaranteed jobs for life. So it makes sense when you are evaluating how to live to think about what you would do if you suffered a reverse. Do you have substantial equity in your house, significant savings or sellable assets? All families should try and develop some form of cushion to help cope with a downfall rather than automatically spend to the limit. Even saving three months' living expenses could prove to be incredibly useful, as it not only provides cash in the hard times but also a breathing space to help you sort the problem out.

All possessions require time and attention. They often require money to maintain them as well. Thus too many of the wrong kind of possessions can demand so much from us that they can harm our relationships with family and friends. We also need to remember that we are not in some sort of competitive battle and do not have to acquire something just because someone else down the road has just bought one. Many people have suffered financially because they tried and failed to 'keep up with the Joneses'. It has been said that this is an impossible task anyway, because 'just about the time you catch up with them, they remortgage their home and go ever deeper into debt in order to buy more things'!

So stick to what is comfortable and most suitable for your family. It is so easy in this society to feel dissatisfied and think that if only we had more, life would be so much better or we'd be happier. But given that most family friction takes place because of money problems, it is vital not to over-commit yourself. We need to remember that we live in one of the most affluent cultures the world has ever known and that we are constantly being bombarded with costly advertising whose prime purpose is to get us to spend money on a particular product. Advertisers usually stress the importance of image rather than function. For example, advertisements for cars rarely focus on their reliability or the fact that they are cheap to run. A car is much more likely to be portrayed as a sex or status symbol.

We can so easily get carried along by the speed of the world today. When we stop and think about some of the things we spend our money on, we must surely ask why. It doesn't seem to matter what the product is – clothes, cars, drink, toilet paper. You name it – and the message that is being communicated is that there is a fulfilling, beautiful, wrinkle- and trouble-free life out there. All we have to do is buy it. Why, many of us will even pay more for sweatshirts and trainers if the manufacturer's label is clearly visible. And if *we* succumb to this pressure, think what impact it has on our teenagers! So many of us can easily end up buying things we don't need with money we don't have to impress people we don't even like!

Unless we are careful we too will get sucked into a world of discontent, envy and coveting. From time to time all of us will get hooked on something we think we must buy. In a man's case it's often a house or car, in a woman's it's more often fashion or household accessories. Once hooked it is very easy to rationalise a purchase. Whatever your plan, do this in the light of your budget and also in full agreement with your partner. Then at least the 'I told you so' syndrome can never come into play.

To determine your standard of living, therefore, you need to sit down with your partner and plan what you want it to be from a realistic viewpoint. Within this you may have both immediate plans and long-term goals. Have a look at an example below.

Richard's and Judy's planned standard of living

We are both concerned about over-extending ourselves and taking on commitments that we would struggle to pay if things went wrong – for example, if Richard lost his job. In fact we would rather live comfortably now and save for the future, both because, ideally, Richard would like to retire early but also because we have our daughter Jane to help through university in a few years' time. We therefore have no intentions of moving to a larger or more expensive home. Rather we want to clear the mortgage as soon as possible and also put money aside regularly in a savings scheme. We will only change our car every seven years and will continue our policy of buying a low-mileage, two-year-old used car as a replacement. We want to look smart but at the same time do not want to waste money by following fashion fads too closely.

Once you have agreed on your family's standard of living you can move on to discuss and then establish your financial goals. This will help you determine your financial priorities. It will also give you something to aim at as a family. In addition you will be able to refer to it in the future to help you weigh up whether any planned major spending actually fits in with your family's priorities.

The best way to start is probably to prepare your own individual goal sheets and then, after comparing the two, produce a family sheet on which you both agree. Remember that some of these goals may be very long term. Just because your present circumstances make them look unlikely, do not limit them or even fail to include them in your plans. Once you have produced your list of goals put them in an agreed order of priority. Ask yourselves which really are the most important. Almost certainly you will not be able to accomplish all your goals at once. In some cases you may not even be able to start preparing straight away. For example, it may not be possible to set aside any extra for retirement until after your children have left college.

Next, draw up a list of your goals for the coming year. What do you want to happen? How are you going to achieve it? Try and be realistic here. Setting unattainable goals in the first year will only lead to anger and frustration and a likelihood of dropping your planning at the first stage. You will need to review this regularly to ensure both that your goals are being met and that other priorities are then moved into a position where they can be tackled next.

Over the longer term you need to ask yourselves some harder questions. How much does your family need in the future? How much should you save? How much do you need to be giving to your children? Ways of doing this are looked at later in this book but at this stage you need to be defining what you want to do.

To help you, have a look at Eamonn's and Anthea's financial goals.

Eamonn's and Anthea's Financial Goals

Date: 1/6/97

Debt Repayments

We would like to reduce and eventually pay off the following:

Car loan	£3,000
Credit cards	£1,000
Mortgage	£30,000

N.B. We intend to reduce the latter by making one extra monthly payment each year.

We also intend not to take out any new credit agreements.

Giving

We currently aim to give 5 per cent of our income to worthy causes, and to increase this over the next five years by 1 per cent p.a. so that we are giving 10 per cent in five years' time.

Lifestyle

We would like to make the following purchase:
Double-glazed windows for the front of the house: £1,000.

Savings

We wish to save 5 per cent of our income and increase this over the next five years by 1 per cent p.a. so that we are saving 10 per cent in five years' time.

Goals for the year 97/8
1 Reduce car loan by £1,000
2 Reduce credit cards by £500.
3 Reduce mortgage by £500 more than required
  (1 extra payment).
4 Increase giving by 1 per cent.
5 Increase saving by 1 per cent.

This is an extra commitment of £2,400 a year and means that there will need to be an extra allocation out of our income of £200 each month in order for this to be achieved.

As you are considering your standard of living there are probably two areas that you need to focus on immediately, as they both have a dramatic impact – housing and cars.

5

HOUSING AND CARS

BUYING A HOUSE

In nearly all homes housing and related costs will be the largest item by a long way. Many families will have bought homes they couldn't really afford at the time in the hope that the houses would rapidly become sharply appreciating assets. However, events of the last decade have seen heavy fluctuations in both interest rates and house prices. When that is coupled with significant job uncertainty, you can see why so many who bought houses with so many dreams soon became disillusioned and even frightened. Although we are supposed to be living in a 'home-owning democracy' it is not necessary for everyone to be buying their own property. The decision to buy or rent should be based on your family's needs and financial situation rather than on any other pressures.

The first thing you must do when thinking of buying a house is to ensure that it fits into your budget. You must be able to afford your accommodation, otherwise you will place an enormous strain on your family. In fact, the on-going stress could destroy it. Remember, too, that interest rates can fluctuate wildly; if you do not have a mortgage with a fixed rate of interest you will have to allow for the fact that at certain times your monthly mortgage will cost you more than it does initially. This is especially true of low-start mortgages which can come as a very nasty shock when they revert in time to 'normal' interest rates. My advice would be if you can only afford to buy a house by getting a low-start mortgage – don't start!

Buying a house within your current budgeting restraints may well mean that you have to settle for smaller accommodation than you ideally would like, but remember, the less you owe on your mortgage the quicker you can pay it off. This could be of tremendous help to you because it may mean that income is released just at a time when you need it elsewhere – when your children are going through college, for example. It is also surely better to build up to your ideal home and plan for it accordingly than to over-commit yourself prematurely – the danger is that you will have a glimpse of your dream home, but then will either never be able to afford to furnish it or, even worse, have it snatched from you when you fail to maintain your mortgage payments.

Although your financial situation will be the main factor in determining what type of housing you need for your family there will be others that need to be brought into consideration. These include:

- Do you plan to live in the area for a long time? If not, consider whether in fact purchasing a property makes sense at this time.

- Is your job situation secure enough for you to take on a mortgage with confidence?

- Can you afford redundancy and sickness insurance to protect you in case something goes wrong?

- Have you taken into account all the additional expenses of buying the property, i.e. Council Tax and utility costs?

- Are you happy with the locality – its safety, shopping facilities, public transport and schools?

- Do house prices hold their value well in the area where you are thinking of buying or are there lots of houses for sale nearby? If there are, do some more exploring just in case there are rumours or plans of something untoward happening in the neighbourhood – like a new motorway being built, for example.

- Do you think this house will be easy to sell?

Another factor that you need to determine when thinking of buying a house is how big a deposit you can put down. This difference between the value of the property and the amount you borrow on a mortgage is known as 'equity'. So, for example, if you were buying a home for £100,000 and have an £80,000 mortgage you would need to have £20,000 as a cash deposit. The higher the deposit you have, the more cushion you have should something go wrong. In this particular case house prices would have to fall by 20 per cent before all the equity disappeared. This is especially important to bear in mind if you are thinking of paying little or no deposit. In the late 1980s it was relatively easy to borrow 100 per cent of a house's value because prices had been rising sharply and it was assumed they would continue to do so. However, prices actually fell considerably, with the result that many people were left with houses worth not only less than they had paid for them but in some cases significantly less than they had borrowed. Literally millions of people were then unable to move home and many eventually faced repossession. What is more, for many the nightmare did not end there: even after the sale, the mortgage company and their insurers can pursue them for the next twelve years in an attempt to make up the shortfall between the eventual selling price of the house and what was owed on the mortgage at that time.

Negative equity, as this is called, has caused anger, bewilderment and confusion. It has led to overcrowding as families have children and are trapped and unable to move into larger houses. This has also been directly responsible for a significant number of relationship breakdowns. It puts people in an almost impossible position should any emergency occur. I would therefore advise very, very strongly against taking out a 100 per cent mortgage. It really is eminently sensible to save as much as you can before buying a house.

When you make your decision to buy a property you have also to consider whether to buy a new or an older one. There are advantages to both. A new house should be built to quite high specifications and have guarantees against all kinds of things going wrong. On the other hand, with an older house you can see how it has settled into the neighbourhood as well as perhaps being able to get many extras, such as carpets, curtains and light fittings, included in the price. But older houses may also have problems from wear and tear which could mean some unexpectedly high repair bills, so if you are buying an older house it is always worth getting a thorough survey done. Problems with drainage or the roof, for example, could be many times the cost of the survey to get sorted out. These problems may cause you to pull out of the purchase altogether or try and renegotiate a lower price. If, however, you are a family with very good do-it-yourself skills you may well deliberately seek out a house in poor condition that is for sale at a low price. You will obviously need to allow extra funds for materials for repairs and it is always worth checking the foundations, plumbing and wiring so the extent of the problems is fully known before you have committed yourself to purchase the house. Once you know all this, if you possess the skills and feel confident that you can renovate the house yourself you should have a home that you will eventually enjoy (especially as a lot of it will be represented by your own hard work!) and should be able to sell at a reasonable profit, should you ever need to, because of the improvements you have made to it.

Almost certainly the best way to buy a house is to save up

and pay for it with cash, but for most of us this is almost impossible to do in our society unless we are trading down from a much larger house. For most people the best options are to start small and make the house as attractive as possible. Then as both income and house prices increase, sell and buy a larger house.

As has already been said, there are several things you should do before finally committing yourself to a house purchase. Listed below are some helpful hints as to what to look out for.

Some dos:

- DO try and see your chosen location at different times. A neighbourhood can change dramatically at night, weekends or during school holidays. Visiting it at different times will give you a much better idea of what it really is like to live there.

- DO enquire into any vacant land or even allotments nearby. Is there any chance that this could be developed for either housing or industrial use?

- DO remember the practicalities. A country cottage in the middle of summer might appear idyllic but most people have to use public transport on a fairly regular basis. How far are the shops, schools, health centres, train and bus stations? What would you do if your car had to go in for major repairs?

- DO look around. Pollution can make living anywhere horrendous and these days it can come in many different forms. Major roads, railway lines, flight paths, pubs and school playgrounds can all lead to various degrees of noise while rubbish dumps, sewerage works, factories and goods yards could lead to air pollution.

- DO check car parking. These days it can be a tremendous problem. Parking problems can lead to road accidents, car theft and disputes between neighbours. Many roads, which could be main roads or streets full of terraced housing, will not have enough parking space for two-car households, let alone for visitors. This would be especially so if the properties close to you had been converted so that more than one family lived there.

- DO think of the layout of the property in conjunction with the needs of your family. For example, a kitchen at the front of the property means that you are unable to watch small children in the back garden while you are washing up or cooking. Open-plan houses can make smaller homes quite spacious but many may not suit teenagers who are looking for 'space to do their own thing'. Separate living and dining rooms allow different things to take place at the same time but mean that rooms are smaller and invariably darker.

- DO look at safety. The safety of the property is paramount. Winding stairs and widely spaced banisters are dangerous for children. All windows should have locks to help stop children falling out and burglars breaking in! Check the kitchen over to see that there is enough space to cook in comfort. Also remember to check the boiler thoroughly. Badly installed or poorly maintained boilers can produce poisonous gas. Stained appliances nearby or a smell of fumes are warning signs.

- DO ask about the electrical wiring. Be wary of anything more than fifteen year old. Ensure that there are sufficient circuit breakers and electrical sockets for the size of the house.

- DO enquire about fuel bills and ask to see copies of both gas and electricity bills, especially for the winter months. A well-insulated property will cost less to heat but it must have good ventilation to prevent condensation. Front doors that open directly into living rooms and large areas of single-glazed north-facing windows push up heating bills in winter. This last point also impacts on lighting bills as north-facing rooms receive no direct sunlight.

- DO check the garden. Steep slopes, uneven fences and ponds can all be difficult to maintain and at the same time can be dangerous to children. High walls and fences with lockable gates will help prevent both children and animals straying but on the other hand could well shade a smaller garden. North-facing gardens will not receive much direct sunlight. Large trees close to the property can easily cause subsidence.

- DO, if you are buying a leasehold property, look carefully at the way the property is managed. Is there a management company that you can be part of and so help control service charges? If not, beware.

And some don'ts:
- DON'T buy a house without seeking professional advice. Although you can do your own conveyancing without resorting to a solicitor, if anything comes up you are unsure of take legal advice straight away. Equally a home buyer's report, or a full structural survey for an older house, is vital.

- DON'T purchase a property that will attract crime. The position of extensions, porches, garages and drain pipes can often provide an easy climbing route for burglars. Houses that back on to open fields, railway embankments, woods and footpaths are all easier for thieves to break into and escape from. In such circumstances, many insurers would insist on extra security in the shape of window and door locks and/or extra premiums.

- DON'T buy a house or a flat next to a busy road unless you have a really secure place for your children to play at the back.

- DON'T buy a property in need of significant modernisation unless you intend to do it up yourself in your own leisure time – and you should have your family's support on this! It is very easy to start with good intentions only to find work pressures or boredom rapidly preventing you from continuing. At this stage you will probably find that the rest of your family are feeling increasingly frustrated that the work has not been done and this will invariably lead to all kinds of family friction. You may then decide that the only thing you can do is to call in a builder to help complete the work. People often tend to considerably underestimate the work and cost involved in making an older house habitable. You have been warned!

- DON'T purchase a flat in an old building if you are concerned about noise. This is usually far worse in flat conversions with poor sound insulation. Noise from both stairwells and upper flats can be a real nuisance, so if you are thinking of buying such a property make sure the bedrooms and living rooms are away from shared entrances, corridors, lifts, etc.

- DON'T buy a house with a large garden unless you want to spend much of your weekends pulling up weeds and mowing the lawn.

- DON'T buy any leasehold property, especially a flat,

without finding out all about the service charges and how they are assessed. How are future repairs and redecoration of common areas going to be funded? Are you liable for structural repairs, window replacements, lift maintenance? The list could be a long one. If you do not determine all these things – and in nearly all cases it is a good idea to get things in writing from the landlord – then in a few years' time you could be faced with crippling demands that you may well not be able to finance, and having them hanging over your head may make it impossible for you to sell as well.

Mortgages

Long gone are the days when if you applied for a mortgage you would be lent two and a half times your salary and you would have to repay it over twenty-five years at variable interest rates. Although twenty-five years remains the most popular period in which to repay a mortgage, you can in fact have them for longer or shorter times, at variable or fixed rates, at three times joint income or greater, and can even borrow 100 per cent of the value of the property you wish to purchase. In addition there is a whole range of ways of repaying the capital element of the mortgage, including endowment policies and links with Personal Equity Plans (PEPS) and pensions.

Unfortunately this has not made life easier for the average family. Until fairly recently as many as 60 per cent of new mortgages were linked to endowment policies – the idea being that when the period of the mortgage finished the endowment would be cashed in and not only pay off the mortgage but leave a very handy nest egg as well. This worked well assuming reasonably high returns, but for much of the 1990s these were trimmed back to such an extent that in a few cases there were genuine fears that the lump sum available at the end of the period would not be sufficient to pay off the mortgage, let alone leave anything left over. Cynics might argue that endowments sold so well because most people buying them really didn't understand how they worked (after all, at the time they were just thinking about buying their house) and that in any case the insurance salespeople who sold them got their commission up-front. Unlike PEP and pension-related mortgages, endowments are not tax exempt so it is hardly surprising that their returns have not been as high. Whatever the reason, about half of all endowment policies are surrendered or allowed to lapse in the first couple of years as people find they can't afford them and in many cases people will get back only a little of what they have put in.

Here is a rundown of the repayment options currently acceptable to most lenders:

Straight repayment mortgage

This is the traditional mortgage under which you make a level payment (subject to interest rate changes) each month, part representing the payment of interest and the other an element of capital repayment, so that at the end of the term the mortgage is completely repaid.

Endowment mortgage

Commonly oversold by the life insurance industry but still worth considering. You pay only the interest to the lender each month, while the payment of premiums on the endowment funds the repayment of capital at the end of the term. The endowment is designed to pay you a bonus at the end of the mortgage term, after the capital has been repaid to the lender. There are a number of variations available, ranging from full endowments (quite expensive but probably profitable) to 'low-cost' endowments which are more readily affordable.

PEP / Unit Trust / Investment Trust

As an alternative to using an endowment to fund the repayment of capital, it is possible to use virtually any other type of investment that is capable of accepting regular, monthly contributions. The use of a **PEP** (Personal Equity Plan) has the advantage of being relatively tax efficient.

Pension mortgage
Again, the borrower pays only interest to the lender while contributing to a personal pension policy. The thinking here is that the borrower will use the tax-free lump sum payable on retirement to repay the mortgage. The disadvantage to this arrangement is that, unless considerable additional contributions are made during working life, it is possible you will end up with a depleted pension.

Given the above you can see that you need to tread very carefully. An honest independent financial adviser is worth his weight in gold, so if you know one, listen carefully. If you don't, I would propose the following advice:

- If you can find a mortgage with a reasonable long-term interest rate that is fixed, consider it carefully – even if it is marginally higher than the current floating rate. If rates are relatively low and stable, that's fine, but you only have to look back a few years to see that there have been quite a few wild swings of interest rates. At the higher levels these can put a large number of people under an enormous strain and start forcing some into areas with all the pressures that extra penalties and possible house repossession cause. Having fixed rates also enables you to know exactly what each month's payment for housing is going to be, so you can budget far more accurately.

- Have a repayment mortgage. As has been mentioned, there is now a swing back from the endowment mortgage to a repayment mortgage, partly because of recent bad publicity but also because interest rates are relatively low. A repayment mortgage pays back both capital and interest elements over the period of the mortgage and only requires additional basic life cover, which comes quite cheaply. If you wish to save, you can probably find more effective and tax-efficient ways than using an endowment.

- Be wary of low-start mortgages. If you are tempted to take one of these because you currently cannot afford the full repayments, ask yourself honestly if you think you will be able to afford it in a couple of years' time when the rates start to move up. Yes, your income may well increase in the meantime, but it takes real discipline not to allow your spending to rise with your income – and what if your circumstances do change or you start a family or whatever?

- Try and pay thirteen payments each year instead of twelve. Again, this will be hard but the savings will be considerable. By doing this you will probably clear a twenty-five-year mortgage within seventeen years and thus could well save yourself tens of thousands of pounds into the bargain. Certain financial institutions already have arrangements to allow this to happen. It also provides a very useful cushion. For example, if you had been doing this for six years and then you lost your job you could revert to the original terms of the mortgage and thus effectively be six months in credit. This gives a wonderful breathing space either to find that other job or at the very least to fill the gap before benefits start helping to pay your mortgage interest.

- Always take out mortgage protection insurance. Since the government has tightened the rules about paying out Income Support for mortgage interest it is imperative that anyone buying a home takes this insurance to ensure that they are protected against both redundancy and sickness. If you think you can't afford the insurance, then you can't afford the mortgage and should lower your sights until you find a property that meets your requirements.

- Before you even start house-hunting have a think about how much you want to save up for a deposit. Although it can be possible to obtain a mortgage of 100 per cent (i.e. you borrow the full purchase price without putting down a deposit) you will save a lot of money in the long run if you can manage to invest some of your own money initially. As soon as you start thinking about house purchase, even a year or so in advance, try to commit yourself to transferring a regular monthly amount into a savings account. Not only will this provide a useful sum to use as a deposit, but it will also help you to adjust to the regular depletion in your spendable income! Furthermore, there are times when it can be difficult to obtain a mortgage, in which case an established connection with a bank or building society can be a real help. It has been known for some insurance salesmen to suggest to young people thinking of buying a house that they should take out some form of insurance policy as early as possible, and that this will help them obtain a mortgage. This is not such a good idea; the question of whether to take out life assurance plans linked to a mortgage can normally be left until you actually apply for the mortgage. Any savings you accumulate for house purchase should be kept accessible in a suitable deposit account.

- Think carefully about re-financing. If interest rates do fall significantly after you've bought your house then you may well feel tempted to switch to a cheaper lender. But there usually has to be a significant fall before it becomes automatically worthwhile to re-finance. The amount that you would actually be saving needs to be compared to any cost in switching lenders, which could include things like new title searches and fees as well as cancellation charges. If these expenses are taken care of over a relatively short period and you are thinking of staying in your property for some considerable period then it is almost certainly worth re-financing.

- Be very wary about taking out second mortgages. As house prices start to rise so the equity in one's home begins to grow. It is very tempting to try and get hold of this 'paper' profit and use it for something tangible like home improvements. The easiest way of doing this is to take out a second mortgage – but it is also one that is fraught with danger. This is because it will usually be for a relatively significant sum and so your monthly expenditure can rise quite sharply, but also because if something goes wrong they will tend to move much more quickly to repossess you than your original mortgage lender. This happens because charges on your home are rated in order of charge, not on a *pro rata* basis. For example, if you had a house worth £70,000, an original mortgage of £60,000 and a second one of £20,000, the original lender would get his money back in full on the sale of the property while the second lender would only get half his money back (in this case £10,000). So secondary lenders tend to take a much closer look at your on-going situation, and if they see the value of your property declining or your debts mounting up they are likely to try and move quickly. Also, as I've said, people often take out second mortgages for some form of home improvement – although it can often be that they simply need the money to pay their outstanding bills. In either case they need to be careful. First, home improvement loans do not usually qualify for benefit payments should things go wrong and, second, borrowing more money – especially against your major asset, the equity of your home – doesn't solve the problems: if you're struggling financially it just adds to them. It may temporarily give the appearance of an improvement in your financial situation but very soon it will be clear that it has treated only the symptoms and not the cause of the problem. This can only be treated effectively by going back to the budget itself.

- Be aware of the heartache of repossession. Very few people today have a job for life. Over the last few years job losses and fluctuating house prices have led to a steady tide of repossession, with hundreds of thousands of people having to leave the properties they had bought with all their plans and dreams some time before. At the first sign of trouble talk to your lender, make the best offer you can afford and stick to it. Share your feelings with your family, too, as mentioned earlier.

Remember above all, when you are looking at a house, that it should primarily be a home ideally suited for your family and not an investment. They will almost certainly feel far happier living in a small but cosy, comfortable and well-furnished house than in a large one with empty rooms which you cannot afford to heat. Many people still owe money on their mortgage when they retire – aim to be different. And if you feel, after weighing up advice, that it is in your family's best interests to rent rather than buy, just go ahead and do so. After all, it is what's best for your family's current circumstances that matters.

CARS

The age and type of car we drive says so much about us. In our society nearly every family owns at least one car. Many of us plan on changing our car well before we actually *need* a new one. We may simply be fed up with our old one, or think it looks old or out of date. Perhaps it needs some repairs to be put back into good condition. Sadly, it is probably more likely that our friends, neighbours or work colleagues have got newer models than ours and so we are feeling somewhat vulnerable. Of course, cars eventually wear out and have to be replaced but we will often change them ahead of time for emotive rather than rational reasons. When it comes to cars, probably more than for any other range of product, we can fall victim so easily to the hype of the advertising media. Many of us will be persuaded by slick advertising to buy cars that we cannot really afford and to trade in an old one well before its life is over. Those who buy brand-new cars say goodbye to literally thousands of pounds as they drive off the garage forecourt. What is more, once you start buying new it is very hard to justify to yourself moving to a second-hand car. After all, in this society which tells us that success is all about the house we live in and the car we drive, it is akin to failure. We need to remember that advertising constantly plays on our greed, fears and snobbery.

Obviously, there will be some groups of people who use their cars a lot because of their jobs and will therefore need to replace their cars fairly frequently, but most of us change our cars because we want to, not because we need to. Ego and self-esteem often cloud our better judgment. Of course all of us, given the choice, would love to be sitting behind the wheel of a new car but we need to ask ourselves not just if we can really afford it, but also whether buying one is the best stewardship of our family's hard-earned money. Costs including payments, insurance and maintenance for an average new car can often be more than £250 a month. It will not take long for that sort of figure to break many a family budget. Even if this figure is maintained, it could well mean that other essentials such as food or clothing will increasingly have to be bought on credit. Almost imperceptibly the debt spiral is beginning.

I believe that the 'normal' family can easily make do with a good-quality reliable used car. Obviously style, size and appearance will depend on your family's circumstances, but buying such a car will in time save you thousands of pounds in depreciation and running costs.

If you are currently allocating significantly more than 15 per cent of your net available income to your overall motoring expenses then you probably need to think about running a more economical car. Here are a few tips to help you keep your motoring costs in check:

- Establish a repair fund within your budget.

- Have the car maintained regularly or do it yourself.

- Deal with any faults as soon as they happen.

- When replacing your car beware of:
  signs of repairing
  burnt oil in the valves
  knocking sounds
  a dirty exhaust
  any vibrations, especially when braking.
  And don't forget to check tyres, electrics and upholstery as well!

So, to summarise – only buy when you really need to; look for a good-value used car; pay cash whenever you can, and if you have to sell consider doing so privately – you can often improve on 'trade-in' prices.

6
USING CREDIT

Probably the biggest financial problem that people have had in recent years is avoiding the credit explosion. Nearly everyone will have faced severe debt problems or at least know of a close family member or friend who has. The vast majority will have been respectable law-abiding citizens who had absolutely no intention of trying to defraud anyone or of not paying what was due.

What has happened is that there has been a significant shift in the way we think about borrowing money. Until about twenty years ago, if you borrowed money it was thought of as debt – something you would desperately try to pay back before your good name was tarnished. But since then a combination of government, financial institution and advertising pressures have encouraged us to borrow more and more. Why, they've even changed it to a more positive-sounding name – credit. We need to be so careful about the way we handle this – especially when 'unbeatable' offers flood through our letter-boxes at an alarming rate. Credit attracts interest. The more you borrow, the more interest you have to pay. Taking out more credit because you can't make ends meet usually means that in time you will be in an even worse situation, because you are trying to paper over the cracks of your overspending. You are trying to treat a symptom rather than deal with the real cause of the problem.

This is especially true when things do go wrong. The body blow of redundancy can make outstanding commitments which previously appeared reasonable now seem crippling.

Sources of credit which previously were encouraging you to borrow more now want pretty fat repayments. Is there any wonder that 'debt' leads to panic? 'Credit', on the other hand, makes you feel you're somebody special. You must be important, surely, or you would not have been allowed to borrow money in the first place. And as for a Gold Card . . . !

Of course, in reality this is complete nonsense but it is a sad reflection on the egoism that permeates so much of our society. There may well be times in our lives when we will have to borrow but when we do we need to do so responsibly, ensuring that both what we are borrowing for and the rates of interest we are paying are reasonable. Given that there are so many different ways of borrowing we ought perhaps to look at them now.

WAYS OF BORROWING

Bank loans and overdrafts

Whenever you need to borrow, the place where you bank should be your first port of call. Many of us find it difficult or embarrassing to talk about money and sometimes shy away from this sort of personal contact in favour of the more anonymous letter offering us credit. But your bank or building society will nearly always be able to offer you the cheapest credit around, so don't be afraid to arrange a meeting with a senior member of staff. When you go, be prepared. Explain what you want the money for and how long you want it. Try and take a copy of your budget with you so you can demonstrate how you are going to be able to repay the money advanced.

The difference between a bank loan and an overdraft is that a loan is taken out over a set period (of, say, three years) and is due to be fully repaid within that time, whereas an overdraft simply enables you to spend more than you actually have in your current account. Typically you would take out a bank loan for the purchase of something like a car or a conservatory. Remember, the longer the loan the more interest you will end up paying, so borrow for the least period of time necessary. If you need to go overdrawn it is essential you get your bank's approval before you do so, otherwise not only will you be facing punitive interest rates but you are also likely to be charged a sum (typically £25) every time one of your cheques is 'bounced'.

It is worth remembering that a bank loan usually works out cheaper than an overdraft and also has a time limit to help you work towards clearing the debt. If the bank turns you down there are always other places you can go to borrow money, but perhaps you should be asking yourself if this isn't a good indication not to borrow the money in the first place.

Credit cards

There are tens of millions of credit cards in use in Britain today. They are very convenient. They are, however, like store cards, very much of a two-edged sword: because they are so easy to use it can often feel as though you're not actually paying money for something you buy with one. Having a credit card means you can spend as much as you like on whatever you like as long as you do not exceed your arranged credit limit. Often, however, you may find that rather than getting a warning letter as you approach your limit you get one telling you that your limit has just been raised substantially!

Credit card companies will build up a picture of you when they consider your credit level. Some of the factors that they will look at include:

- Do you own your own home or are you renting?

- How long have you lived there?

- Your job and your level of remuneration

- How long have you worked there?

Once they have considered these and other points they will decide what repayments they think you can afford (although strangely they do not seem to take into account other credit repayments you may be making).

Many people argue that they use credit cards because they can provide several weeks of 'free' credit. This is because when your statement arrives with a sum outstanding on it there is also a date for repayment. If you then pay all that you owe so that it arrives on or before that date you should be charged no interest. This can effectively mean you can borrow for five or six weeks, interest free. However, it is not quite that simple. First, as has been said, using credit cards doesn't feel like spending money so the temptation is that we will spend more just by having them. Second, if we do not pay off all the outstanding amount each month we will be charged interest, often at quite high rates, on the whole amount owing. If we keep going in this way, the following month the interest charge received in month one will itself have interest charged on it. Go on for any period of time and a large amount of what you owe is in fact accumulated interest!

So unless you handle your finances well and can resist the credit temptations you need to be wary about the use of credit cards. Over 50 per cent of people in Britain who have them do not pay them off every month and are thus accruing unnecessary interest.

Store cards

These work in the same way as credit cards but sometimes they charge an even higher rate of interest. People are often persuaded to take out store cards from shops they go to fairly regularly – there are often initial discounts to tempt you to do so. These discounts are not just offered because the stores are feeling generous. Once you have filled in an application form for one of their cards the store has a fairly accurate picture of what you're like and what you're likely to spend your money on! They will thus be able to send you regular offers of things that you always seem to want. As with credit cards, only take up the offer of store cards if you possess an iron will, are able to take advantage of the discounts offered because you were going to make the purchase anyway, and are determined not to be pressured into buying anything else.

Hire purchase

Hire purchase is nothing like as common as it used to be before credit was relaxed. Previously you would probably have had to put down a fairly significant deposit (perhaps one-third) before you could buy goods on HP. Nowadays no deposit is needed. The main difference between other forms of borrowing and hire purchase is that with other forms of borrowing the goods belong to you straight away, whereas with HP they become legally yours only when you have finished paying for them. If for some reason you stop paying for the goods, they can be repossessed if you have paid less than one-third of the total or you can be taken to court to pay the balance. Hire purchase is usually significantly more expensive than borrowing directly from your bank and can be particularly hard if your circumstances change for the worse fairly early on during the agreement, because you may lose both your goods and the money you've paid.

Interest-free credit

Today there is a whole range of inducements to buy goods – including interest-free credit. The cost of credit always has to be paid in some way. There really is no such thing as a 'free lunch'. If you are buying a substantial item with interest-free credit you should be able to negotiate a significant discount for cash. Even if you can't, you need to be careful. It is quite easy to celebrate what you think is a good deal by going out and blowing the cash you had saved up for the item on something else.

Catalogues

Many people who buy goods through catalogues pay for the items they purchase on a monthly basis. It usually costs quite a lot to do this and the likelihood is that during the time you're paying the new catalogue will arrive and you will be tempted to get carried away and buy items you don't really need. Catalogue debts are often a major problem – especially with lower-income families.

Authorised money-lenders

It may surprise you to know that there are still several millions of people in Britain who have loans that they repay every week to people who come knocking on their door. Usually these are people who have not 'scored' highly enough to get bank, building society or credit card facilities. As such they may well be relatively poor and borrowing for essentials rather than luxuries. Even though they can least afford it they will be being charged very high rates of interest.

Unauthorised money-lenders (or loan sharks)

Some people live in such dire circumstances that when they have to borrow from someone they will usually end up borrowing from loan sharks. Loan sharks usually operate locally and offer their 'services' to these vulnerable people. They normally offer relatively small amounts at extortionate rates to help families eat, keep warm and have enough for the kids at Christmas. Nearly all these people operate illegally, can intimidate if they don't get repaid on time and will charge excessively. Sadly, interest rates of 1,000 per cent are not unheard of. Not surprisingly once you are hooked into this sort of arrangement it is almost impossible to get out. Whatever you do and however desperate your need, please try and find an alternative way of borrowing.

Credit Unions

An increasing number of Credit Unions are appearing in

Britain. To join one you need to have a common bond with the other members – so your church, neighbourhood, workplace or union, for example, might run one. Because they are run for a common purpose and usually locally, there are few expenses and thus the differential in interest rates between borrowing and saving can be very low. In effect the 'better-off' members of a Credit Union are helping the poorer members borrow at a cheaper rate than they would be able to do elsewhere – without necessarily taking lower interest themselves. For more details about Credit Unions contact the Association of British Credit Unions (ABCUL) whose address can be found at the end of this book.

Secured or unsecured loans
One of the main factors in determining the rate of interest you will be charged when you borrow is whether your loan is secured against something or not. A secured loan is when you offer an asset as security to the lending organisation. The most common example of this would be a mortgage on your home, but it could also apply, for example, if you purchased a car with a loan. In either case the asset can be forcibly repossessed by the lender or at least they can make you sell the asset in order that the amount you borrowed (sometimes with added interest and penalties) can be reclaimed.

The advantage of a secured loan is that it usually is at a much lower rate of interest than an unsecured loan. The disadvantages, though, are huge. You can lose your major assets if you fail to maintain the payments on such loans.

In most daily newspapers it is quite common to see adverts along the lines of 'put all your debts in one basket'. It is obviously very tempting for many to think of making just one debt payment a month instead of many, particularly if it is at a lower rate of interest. However, in very small print these adverts usually say, 'Your home is at risk if you do not keep up with your repayments'.

Therefore, unless you have got your spending under strict control you run the risk not only of seeing your debts continue to mount but also of losing your major asset. So think long and hard before you put the security of your family's home at risk.

DEBIT CARDS

One way of having the advantages of carrying a card around rather than lots of cash is to use a debit card such as Switch. Their usage has been increasing significantly in recent years. By using a debit card you pay for the goods in the same way as with a credit card but the amount charged is immediately (sometimes the same day, though usually the following one) debited to your bank account. This obviously makes you think twice, because money is in effect coming out of your account immediately and so you need to determine both whether you need something and whether you can afford it. The fact that you cannot spend more than is in your account is a good reminder to handle your card spending carefully and therefore the sensible usage of debit cards can be recommended.

So when it comes to credit you have to decide how often you're going to use it and in what way. Just because you can borrow doesn't mean that you should – even though that is what society tells you. Before you make any firm decisions ask yourself questions such as:

- Do I really need this item?

- Do I need it now?

- What benefit/pleasure will it bring me/my family?

- Has advertising/peer pressure played a part in this decision?

- Can I delay buying this until I can afford to pay cash for it?

- Will this purchase increase my levels of credit to dangerous levels?

If in doubt, hesitate and review your decision in a couple of weeks. You may well find you have changed your mind by that time!

7
DEBT

Given how easy it now is to get credit it is not surprising that there have been an enormous number of casualties. If you are in debt or even fearing that you are about to slip into it, take action straight away. The quicker you act the sooner you will be able to put your problems behind you. Do not just sit around hoping that a cheque will appear in the post – it almost certainly will be another bill. And however hopeless it seems, things can get better. There are people who can help you at your local Citizens' Advice Bureau or you can ring Credit Action (0800 591084).

One of the first things they will do is look at your budget without including any loan/debt repayments in it so that they can see what you can afford to pay towards your total debts each month. Then there is a need to separate your secured debts from your unsecured. As we have just seen, when looking at credit it is imperative to try and maintain payments on secured loans or you have the real risk of losing that asset. The penalties for not paying unsecured debts are not as great, though you could still go to court, get fined and find that you have been banned from having further credit. In other words, it is more important to pay your mortgage than your credit card because of the penalties involved – but you still need to be talking to your credit card companies and making realistic offers to them.

Remember that debt rarely strikes in isolation and so you may be facing other pressures as well. Talk to your partner about the debt problems the family are facing. Try and come up with a joint strategy for resolving them and if you need to seek advice go together. There are three key things that you need to do:

- **Be realistic** Don't gloss over the problems and don't look at your debt in isolation. You need to face up to the whole picture.

- **Act responsibly** It is important for your family that you do this and do not try to avoid making payments or contacts when you could. Creditors normally write several times before legal action is threatened. You cannot blame them for getting annoyed if their letters are not answered or if promises are made and then broken with no explanation.

- **Take action** Every week you do nothing the amount of money you owe will be going up as interest accumulates. Not facing up to debt also causes enormous family friction, anger and abuse and, sadly, far too often leads to the breakdown of the whole unit. It can cause health problems, loss of friends and depression for you and for others in your family, so don't be too proud to take advice. You may well have made mistakes, but then who hasn't? One thing you could do straight away is cut up any credit cards you may be using and return them to the credit card company. At the same time enclose a copy of your budget and make an offer on the basis of it, asking them to freeze the interest. After all, there is little point in you paying them £20 a month if they are charging you £30 a month interest! They may be reluctant to agree to this at first, but when they appreciate that you are struggling but trying to resolve the situation they should be more sympathetic. Interest is also frozen once a judgment has been made in court, so if they believe your budget it could be in their interest to agree to this as well.

Many people struggling with debt do not claim all the benefits they are entitled to. Again, this is something that the Citizens' Advice Bureau can help you with. If you do decide to go to the Benefits Agency remember to have a complete family picture of your circumstances when you go. If you are looking after an aged granny or have a handicapped child, for example, there probably will be additional benefits for you. In any case it is always worth asking – you certainly won't get any more if you don't. Unfortunately government cut-backs mean there is no longer a freephone helpline for benefits advice so you will have to find details of your local benefits agency by looking in the phone book.

CREDIT REFERENCE AGENCIES

If you have been struggling with debt and particularly if you have a county court judgment against you this will be recorded on your credit reference file. Virtually everyone in this country has such a file and whenever anyone applies for credit the retailer, bank, etc., will normally contact the credit reference agency they use (there are three or four main ones) for details about you. The file will give details of your home, address, how long you've lived there and other details including whenever you've applied for credit. In addition it will have records of any court action taken against you for non-payment and could even have notice of the fact that you have paid some creditors far too slowly for their liking.

Under the Consumer Credit Act you have the right to know what is being said to you. The procedure is as follows:

1 Ask the retailer to give you the name and address of the agency they consulted within twenty-eight days of them doing so.
2 The retailer must reply within seven working days.
3 Once you have the name and address write to the agency and ask for your file, enclosing a £1 fee. Give as

    much information as you can to help them trace you.

4 The agency must reply within seven working days, enclosing a copy of your file if they have one.

5 Check it thoroughly. If there are mistakes in it (and sometimes there are!) ask them to correct them.

6 The agency should then reply within twenty-eight days. If things have not been amended to your satisfaction you can write a short note of correction (under 200 words) and ask them to include it in your file. As long as your correction is honest they should add it to your report.

7 If the agency either corrects your file itself or adds your statement to it, they must send the correction to anyone who has asked about your credit rating in the last six months. Equally they must refer to the correction in the future.

8 If you cannot get satisfaction you can demand arbitration.

Your files are very important. If you are subject to a bad credit reference it makes it incredibly difficult for you to get any new credit facilities (and sometimes this will even include bank accounts) for six years. So, for example, if you had a county court judgment (CCJ) against you in January 1997 it would be February 2003 before it disappeared from your file and you could get credit again. If, however, you do get a CCJ and pay it after that time, the fact that you have done so will be stated on your file but the judgment itself will *not* be removed, unless payment is made within twenty-eight days of the judgment taking place.

NEGOTIATING WITH CREDITORS

During the course of getting out of debt you will need to negotiate with all your creditors. You will undoubtedly get differing reactions from some of them, but despite that there are some guidelines that you should use in dealing with them:

1. **Always treat the creditor with respect**. The people you are dealing with are just doing their jobs. Always stay polite, however hard it is, even when they are being antagonistic towards you. This, of course, does not mean that you have to agree with everything they say.
2. **Stay calm**. You will not always reach agreement with your creditors straight away. You need to stay calm but firm. Losing your temper or criticising the creditor will do your cause no good at all.
3. **Acknowledge your creditor's limitations**. Many of the people you will be dealing with have certain boundaries within which they can operate and be flexible. Trying to get them to do something beyond this will prove impossible. This, of course, is a very good reason for trying to deal with a senior person who has maximum flexibility.
4. **Explain the benefits of your proposal to the creditor**. Sometimes you can make suggestions which would be mutually beneficial. One example of this would be if your home was threatened with repossession and you suggested you stayed in it until it was sold. This would be beneficial to you as you would be in your home longer and therefore have breathing space to make alternative arrangements. Equally the building society is likely to get a higher price, with lower costs, if you stay and try and sell the property rather than leave it empty.
5. **Stick to what you say**. Once an agreement has been reached on the maximum you can pay to each creditor, start the payments and keep to them. Whatever you do, don't pay a creditor more because he kicks up a fuss.

There will be times when negotiation fails and at that stage you can expect your case to go to court. Even if this does happen do not despair. Courts are not there automatically to punish you. They are there to assess what is fair. In any case, because there are often several million summonses for debt each year, many of these cases are now dealt with by letter rather than people actually having to appear. It is vital in either case that all forms sent to you by the court are filled in honestly and accurately and that if you are called to appear in court you attend. Failing to do so, and sadly a very large number of people do just that, will mean that judgment is automatically found against you.

If your situation means you are facing court action, may have visits by bailiffs or are even facing bankruptcy, it is important you take professional advice. For example, some of the laws regarding what bailiffs can and can't do are extremely complex, so seek advice from your local Citizens' Advice Bureau, solicitor or insolvency practitioner.

To summarise, if your family is struggling with debt here are some tips to help you begin to see light at the end of the tunnel.

What to do

- DO admit all your debts.

- DO acknowledge that this could affect you and your other family members emotionally.

- DO talk to the rest of the family about the problems straight away.

- DO seek advice wherever necessary.

- DO communicate with all your creditors and keep a copy of all correspondence.

- DO check whether you have any benefit entitlement.

- DO draw up your budget, excluding any debt/loan

repayments, so you can see what, if anything, can be allocated to this.

- DO distinguish between priority and non-priority creditors.

- DO make offers to your creditors that are realistic and stick to them.

- DO seek advice again if you are threatened with court action or bailiffs.

What not to do
- DON'T put your head in the sand and simply hope the problems will disappear.

- DON'T fail to tell your family what is happening.

- DON'T refuse to open the post and ignore any court summons.

- DON'T be rude to creditors.

- DON'T fail to check your benefits.

- DON'T merely guess at where your money is going.

- DON'T buy non-essentials when essentials have not yet been paid for.

- DON'T make offers to creditors you know that you can't afford.

- DON'T cut yourself off from your family and friends.

8

GIVING

If your family has decided to give to charity some useful tax concessions are available. The tips contained in this chapter will help you bring maximum benefit to those you want to help – be it a regular gift to your local church, a response to an emergency appeal or even a legacy in your will. You can gain some income tax relief through regular giving under covenant and also through payroll-giving schemes. Gift Aid also enables you to give bigger one-off gifts to charity in a tax-efficient way. Taxation is dealt with in full in chapter 11.

Your first decision as a family is to establish your giving priorities. The choices of giving are almost endless – church, emergency relief, poor countries, individual sponsorship and a whole range of national and international charities – and it is likely that there will be differences of opinion as to where your money should go. It is always a good idea to do some research into charities before you decide to give to them. For example, you might want to know how much of what you give actually goes to meet the needs concerned compared with advertisements and fund-raising costs. It is also important that all members of the family learn to appreciate the benefits of your giving, and this is especially so for the younger children. For example, this could be demonstrated in a small way by giving cans of food to a hostel for the homeless. Once the benefits have been fully recognised it makes sense to find ways that these can be maximised. Some of these are listed below.

Covenants to charity

You can get tax relief at your highest rate of tax on all payments you make to registered charities under a deed of covenant. A deed of covenant is a legally binding agreement in which you agree to make a series of payments – although should your circumstances change dramatically for the worse (e.g. you lose your job and can no longer afford to maintain them) you are allowed to cancel without any penalty to yourself. In order to get the tax relief on these payments they should last for at least three years.

There are few exceptions about claiming tax relief and giving to charities. The main one is that if you were to get a significant benefit from the tax relief yourself, you would not be able to claim tax relief. So, for example, you could not use a covenant to pay your child's school fees if he went to a private charitable school. Smaller benefits, however, such as reduced entrance prices, would enable you to covenant.

A covenant works in the following way. If you are a regular tax-payer you hand over a net amount as a gift, and the charity can reclaim the tax deducted so it ends up with the gross amount of your gift. In effect this process is automatically giving you basic tax relief. You will have to claim this on your tax return and you will receive it either through an adjusted PAYE figure or in a reduced tax bill.

Because tax rates can change from year to year it is sensible to agree to give a fixed net amount each year, although this could mean that what the charity actually receives could vary from year to year.

Most charities make it easy to give in this way by having special covenant forms printed. These are usually over a four-year period, to meet the 'over three years' rule. The form will need to be both signed and witnessed before it can be used. Although a covenant may be drawn up to run for just the four years, you will continue to get tax relief if you maintain your payments for longer than that time.

Payroll-giving schemes

If your employer has an approved payroll-giving scheme you can get tax relief at your highest rate on donations to charity up to certain limits. The money goes to the charities of your choice and you do not need to draw up a covenant or agree to pay for a minimum period. There are limits on the amount you can give each year but these have risen quite generously in the last few years. To get your tax relief your employer must have set up a payroll-giving scheme (commonly known as 'Give As You Earn'). This in effect means they have to sign up with an agency approved by the Inland Revenue, which then collects money employees wish to give and passes it on to the relevant chosen charities. The money you want to give is deducted from your pay prior to your tax being assessed, which therefore automatically gives you tax relief.

Gift Aid

You can also get tax relief at your highest rate on single one-off gifts to charity, provided they are over a certain figure. Once above that figure there is no limit to how much you can give and claim tax relief for. Gift Aid works very similarly to covenants when it comes to tax relief, so if you are a higher rate tax-payer you are entitled to relief at the highest rate for all the gift. If you do use Gift Aid you should provide the charity with a tax deduction certificate. They will probably be able to give one of these to you. If not, they are available from your local tax office.

Inheritance tax

Gifts and legacies to UK registered charities are completely free of inheritance tax regardless of how large they are. What is more, if you owned an asset which otherwise would incur significant capital gains tax you could give it to a charity and there would be no tax to pay at all. On the other hand, if you owned something at a loss it would be better to sell it and give the proceeds to the charity, thus enabling you to offset your loss against your chargeable gains. Certain other gifts which would be perceived as being 'for the public benefit' can also be given to non-profit-making organisations without incurring any tax penalty.

9
SAVINGS

If you have some capital, no matter how small, it's worth knowing about the different types of investment available. Sometimes the choice can be quite overwhelming.

BANKS AND BUILDING SOCIETIES

This is where you start. It is difficult to survive the modern world without a bank or a building society account. Some folk do try, preferring to deal in cash at all times, but this is not a serious option for most people.

You will probably want to have a current account that provides you with a cheque book. (We call it a current account in the UK; the Americans prefer to call it a checking account. They amount to the same thing.) Although a current account is fine for everyday transactions, this is not the best place to leave money you have no immediate use for. Few current accounts pay interest on the money you leave there, and those that do pay interest do so at a very low rate.

The first step towards accumulating some savings will be to open either a separate bank deposit account or a building society account. Even this type of account is unlikely to pay a particularly high level of interest, but it will be a start. If you are thinking of buying your first home and want to save up so that you will have a reasonable deposit to put on the house of your choice, a regular payment into some form of deposit account is ideal.

OTHER WAYS TO INVEST

It is important to have some idea of other savings and investment products available. Even if you have no money to invest now, it is possible the following information will come in useful later in life.

National Savings

All National Savings investments pay gross interest although, as a general rule, the interest has to be declared on a tax return. So there may be income tax to pay.

Ordinary account

This is designed for the smaller deposit, and only pays low rates of interest. As well as paying gross interest, a small sum is free of tax even if your income exceeds your personal allowance.

Investment account

This has a variable rate of interest, depending on the amount invested. Interest is credited annually, so it is not suitable if you require a regular income.

Income bonds

These rates will change from time to time during your investment. Income is paid gross, every month. Three months' notice is required for withdrawal (or three months' lost interest for immediate access).

Pensioners' bonds

Interest is payable gross, fixed for five years regardless of changes in interest rates generally. Sixty days' notice for withdrawal within the five-year period, and no interest paid during this period of notice.

All of the above have different minimum and maximum investments, so to find out more about these, and other National Savings products, enquire at any Post Office or by post to:

> National Savings
> FREEPOST BJ2092
> Blackpool
> FY3 9XR

or by telephone on 0645-645 000 (charged at local rates).

Tax-Exempt Special Savings Accounts (TESSAs)

A TESSA is, as its name implies, tax free but you must keep the money invested for five years – otherwise you will be taxed – and you can only invest up to a certain sum each year. Most banks and building societies operate these accounts, and although the rate of interest varies from one place to another, you should be able to obtain a rate that is better than an ordinary deposit account.

It is possible to draw the income from a TESSA each year, although there will be a deduction for income tax which will only be refunded to your account once you have successfully completed the full five-year term.

At the end of the five years you are guaranteed the return of all capital invested, plus any interest not already taken. However, beware: some TESSA managers are now offering a more speculative version, so before investing make sure your account guarantees your full capital, if that is what you want.

Personal Equity Plans (PEPs)

PEPs are also tax free but are not to be confused with TESSAs, as these two investments are quite different from each other.

PEPs were introduced in the 1986 Budget to encourage individuals to invest in shares. PEPs are run by plan managers, for example a bank or investment company. The PEP's main advantage is the absence of tax on dividends or capital gains.

There is currently a maximum investment per year which can be split between a *general* PEP and a *single-company* PEP. A general PEP will consist of investments in any combination of ordinary shares, qualifying investment trusts or unit trusts. A single-company PEP will be an investment in the ordinary shares of either a UK or EC company. You are entitled to the income from the investments and gains, free of tax.

The most important aspect to appreciate is the risk element. Like any investment in stocks and shares, you never quite know what return you can expect. There is also the possibility that the value of your investment could fall. This might not matter that much if you are prepared to 'sit it out' and wait for the performance to improve – but not every investor has the stomach for such things. If the prospect of seeing the value of your investment fall would be too much for you to take, it would be best to avoid this type of investment in the first place.

Insurance company bonds
Many investors with a lump sum to invest turn to insurance companies for advice, or have insurance products recommended to them by financial advisers. Often, a 'bond' will appear to be the solution – but what exactly is an insurance bond, and what are the differences between the various types of bond on offer? How speculative are they?

Guaranteed income (guaranteed growth) bonds
A guaranteed income bond promises a guaranteed, fixed rate of return, either paid as an income or left to accumulate, with a guarantee that the capital will be returned in full at the end of the contract period. You can currently obtain a fixed rate of interest of approximately 6 per cent net of

basic-rate tax over a three- or four-year period, and it should be possible to receive the income monthly – although not all insurance companies that offer income bonds do, in fact, offer the monthly income facility.

A guaranteed income bond is virtually risk free, as long as you are dealing with an insurance company licensed to trade in the UK. Even if interest rates fall after you have made the investment, you are still locked in to the rate which was agreed at the outset.

While it is good to know you have secured an attractive rate when interest rates generally are falling, this can prove to be a disadvantage if interest rates rise again during your investment. However, this is compensated for by the knowledge that you have a fixed, reliable income coming in no matter what happens.

Investment bonds

This is a much more speculative investment, as your entire capital is being invested by the insurance company across a range of stocks and shares and also, perhaps, property. Although it is possible to arrange for the receipt of a regular income, there is no guarantee at all that the underlying growth in the investment is going to be sufficient to fund the income. Furthermore, there is no guarantee, even if you draw no income from the bond, that your capital will be preserved. If investment conditions are rough, you cannot expect the value of your bond to do anything but follow the general trend downwards.

Some insurance company investment bonds have performed well in recent years, and this is a way of investing in equities without your having to take any active part in the investment decisions yourself. However, this form of investment can prove to be far too speculative for many investors, and it is necessary to take a long-term view and not expect instant profits.

If you are interested in an investment in stocks and

shares, you would probably be better off starting with a PEP.

Other investments

Space does not allow me to cover all investments here, and there are many more available, usually at quite a high risk to capital. For instance, there is nothing to stop you investing in stocks and shares by instructing a stockbroker or investing in unit trusts, investment trusts or government stock (gilts). But the risks can be very high indeed, and you would have to take expert advice.

OBTAINING ADVICE

One of the most difficult, and most important, things to establish is whether an investment adviser is independent or 'tied'. An independent adviser is one who can recommend the investment or life assurance products of a whole range of companies; a 'tied' agent can only deal with the one company (usually an insurance company) which he represents.

To find a suitable adviser, you can try turning to the Yellow Pages under the heading of Financial Advisers, and choose one of the listed firms, as long as they describe themselves as independent. Most of them will be registered with the Personal Investment Authority (PIA). Alternatively, they may be registered for the provision of financial advice through the IBRC (Insurance Brokers' Registration Council). In either case, member firms are tightly controlled, and a compensation scheme exists in the case of default.

Some solicitors and accountants – but by no means all of them – are in a good position to advise on investment matters.

Alternatively, you can call Independent Financial Advisers (IFA) promotions on 0117-971 1177. They will take your address and post you a list of some suitable independent firms in your area.

You should bear in mind that most banks and building societies are 'tied' to one insurance company.

PENSIONS

It is a fact of life that most people don't give much thought to pensions until they are too old to do much about making proper provision. As soon as you start work you should be putting some money to one side for your pension. Although you will probably receive a pension from the state (the so-called 'old-age pension') it is unlikely this will be enough to keep you in the manner to which you have become accustomed!

If you are an employed person and your employer offers you the opportunity of joining a company pension scheme it is almost always a good idea to join. Even if you do have to suffer deductions from your payslip into the pension scheme, your employer will be contributing equal or greater levels each month on your behalf, and there will probably be some life insurance contained in the pension scheme. You can volunteer to make extra payments into the scheme if you want to enhance the amount payable when you reach retirement age. These are known as Additional Voluntary Contributions (AVCs).

There is a particular advantage in using a pension fund for savings – and that is the tax benefit. The government does not tax the profits made by pension funds, so this helps them grow. Furthermore, you obtain tax relief from any pension contributions you make. If there is no company scheme, or you are self-employed, you should consider taking out a personal pension policy. Again, there are tax benefits to investing in this type of policy, including tax relief on all your premium payments up to certain limits. You can also include some life insurance benefits and, again, you obtain tax relief on these premium payments.

There is quite a bewildering choice of different investment funds ranging from staid but secure 'with-profit' policies to 'equity-linked', which are more closely related to the investment performance of shares. It is important you obtain advice from someone qualified to deal with pensions as it is easy to make mistakes.

10
INSURANCE

Insurance is not a subject you're going to get too excited about – unless something goes wrong. Only then are you likely to read your insurance policy to see whether or not you can claim. But this is the wrong way of going about making sure you have the insurance you need.

Once you have acquired some property worth protecting you will need to start making enquiries about insurance. First of all, let's look at some basic principles.

To obtain the protection of insurance you pay a premium. The amount of premium you pay depends on the insurance company's assessment of how likely they are to have to pay a claim. For example, younger drivers pay more for their car insurance than older drivers, because older drivers are going to have more experience, can anticipate problems on the road better than novice drivers can, and are less likely to drive fast to impress their friends!

So the insurance company takes your premium and this is added to the common 'pot' from which claims are paid. Surprisingly, insurance companies often find they pay out more in claims than they receive in premiums, so perhaps they are not quite as hard as many people think. Fortunately, insurance companies have other sources of income to make up the loss, such as the investment income they receive from all the accumulated premium payments, or from interest charged on instalment schemes.

THE PROPOSAL FORM

Around the time you pay your premium you will be asked to complete an application form, known as a proposal form. This is the most important part of the transaction and you have to be extremely careful. In particular, note the following:

Tell the truth, the whole truth and nothing but the truth!
Insurance is based on the principle that it's up to you to tell the insurance company anything that could possibly make a difference to whether or not they will accept you and at what premium. After all, you know all about yourself, and you can't expect the insurance company to be aware of all the facts unless you tell them. If you fail to disclose some important information, this can quite easily count against you later on if you have to make a claim.

This is easily illustrated by an example. There is a question on your car insurance proposal form that asks if you have ever had a previous accident. You forget all about that embarrassing occasion when you drove into the back of the car in front of you, so you answer the question in the negative. Some time later you have another accident and your insurance company gets to know about the previous one, even though you never mentioned it on the form. The insurance company is quite justified in turning down your claim, leaving you with the costs of repairing your own car.

Think carefully about the cover you need
If you intend to drive your car in connection with your job from time to time, but only ask for social and pleasure use, you will not obtain the cover you need.

Put them in the picture
Tell the insurance company anything you think might be relevant, even if there is no specific question covering this

on the proposal form. This way, you will minimise any possibility of the insurance company complaining that you have held anything back.

Bear in mind that when you apply for insurance you are entering into a legally binding contract that requires both parties to the contract (i.e. both you and the insurance company) to be open and honest. If you keep to your obligations under the contract you can expect the insurance company to do likewise if you have to claim.

CAR INSURANCE

This is most people's first introduction to insurance, partly because it is compulsory – you are not allowed to drive a car on the road without it. There are three types of cover available:

Third party only
The term 'third party' refers to anyone who has cause to claim against you because of any fault on your part. So if you drive your car into a neighbour's car, and then go on to demolish his garden wall too, it is only reasonable to expect that he will look to you for reimbursement. Third-party insurance will cover you for this and will pay to have your neighbour's property repaired, so long as he can establish that it really was your fault. Third-party cover will only pay out if you can be shown to be legally responsible. It is this cover that is compulsory and will also apply for any personal injury you may cause.

Third party, fire and theft
As well as being covered for third-party claims, you will be able to claim for any damage caused to your car arising out of fire or theft (obvious really!). Although the car will be covered for fire damage, this will not cover you for any mechanical failing, as the insurance is not intended to act as a maintenance contract. If, for example, your car caught fire because

of some faulty wiring, you would be able to claim for the damage caused by the fire, but not for the cost of rewiring!

Comprehensive

Here you are covered for third party together with damage caused to your own car regardless of the cause. So you would be able to claim for damage caused to your car arising out of an accident, and you can also claim for more routine damage, such as scraping the car on the garage door. But every time you claim you risk losing your no claims bonus (see below). A comprehensive policy also contains some additional benefits that are not all that important, but can come in useful on occasion. You will normally be covered for the loss of personal effects up to £100 or so and there will also be some 'personal accident' benefits in the event of injury. But the level of cover will be low, and if you really want to have insurance that pays out for injury, you should make separate arrangements.

Once you have selected the type of cover you want, you need to have a think about what you're going to be using the car for, as this can make a considerable difference to the premium you pay.

Classes of use

Social, domestic and pleasure use

This is the least expensive class and is normally sufficient for most domestic motoring. Although it does not include any business use, it does allow you to use the car for travel from your home to your regular place of work.

Class 1

This includes business use, but only by the policyholder in person. It does not include business use for any other driver. It will not include commercial travelling (i.e. going from place to place in search of business).

Class 2
As class 1, but it allows other drivers to use the car for business.

Class 3
This allows commercial travelling.

These classes of use can be very confusing. If you are not too sure which one you need, you should take advice. Just explain exactly what you wish to use the car for, and your adviser should be able to arrange the right cover for your circumstances.

Accidents
Having an accident can cause great upset, even without insurance problems. It is important to know what you should do following an accident. Here are a few points to follow:

- **Always stop**. If you leave the scene of an accident without providing your details to anyone else involved, you are committing a criminal offence.

- **Make a note of the registration numbers of any other cars whether they were involved directly or indirectly**. For example, it is possible for a car to cause an accident without actually coming into contact with you.

- **Ask for the names and addresses of anyone else involved**.

- **Did anyone else see what happened?** Try to get names and addresses, as an independent witness can be a great help if you are wanting to establish that the accident was someone else's fault.

- **Make it your business to establish if anyone has been**

injured. If there has been some injury the police have to be informed immediately.

- **Try not to enter into discussion concerning who's at fault**. Whatever you do say, do not admit liability and don't ever sign any statements at the scene of the accident.

- **Once you have completed your journey (if you can) contact your insurance company for help**.

No claims bonus

Although it is very welcome to be rewarded with a no claims bonus (or discount) if you don't make any claims, this system does introduce some stress into the relationship with your insurance company. For every year without claim, your bonus is increased up to a maximum of approximately 65 per cent. In most cases, once you have reached the maximum bonus, you lose only part of it if you have to claim. But having two claims in one year or fairly close to each other usually means you lose all the bonus and you have to start again.

The reason this causes so much stress is that you can only retain your bonus entitlement if your insurance company can recover the amount of the claim from whoever was responsible. Clearly, this is a forlorn hope if you simply drove your car into a lamp-post and you have no one to blame but yourself! But even if you think an accident was someone else's fault, proving it is another matter. For example, accidents on roundabouts, with various cars aiming for numerous different exits, are notoriously difficult to prove one way or the other. One car hits the other, and each driver is convinced it was the other's fault. Unless there is an independent witness who can support your version of events, it is highly unlikely your insurance company will be able to recover the cost of your repairs from the other motorist's insurer – in which case you will lose all or part of your bonus, even though you are convinced of your own innocence.

If this happens, don't get cross with your insurance company. It's not their fault.

Sometimes you will have 'uninsured' losses. This might be a policy excess or perhaps you have hired a car while your own has been in for repairs. If you think you can pin the blame for the accident on the other motorist, you should write to him and ask him to pass your letter on to his insurance company. If you succeed in obtaining payment for your uninsured losses, do tell your own insurance company, as this will be evidence that your no claims bonus should be reinstated. If you have an insurance broker, he will probably look after the claiming of uninsured losses on your behalf, or he might have arranged for you to be included in an 'accident recovery' service which prevents you having to deal with all the correspondence.

Motor claims are a messy business. If you can manage to avoid coming into contact with other cars you will save yourself a lot of bother!

HOME CONTENTS INSURANCE

Not everyone bothers to insure their home contents and other belongings, but opting out can be an expensive mistake, especially if you are ever sued!

Example
You are leaving a department store and, as you join the throng on the street, you realise it is raining. In the process of putting up your umbrella, you succeed in poking the end in someone's eye. The injured woman is extremely upset and demands to know your name and address, which you feel you have no option but to provide. 'You will be hearing from my solicitor!' is her parting shot.

Some weeks later you do indeed receive a solicitor's

letter, in which it is stated that the woman is in danger of losing the sight of the damaged eye. She is expecting a substantial payment in compensation.

You would be stuck if you didn't have any home contents insurance. That might sound strange, but almost all home contents policies automatically provide personal liability insurance. If you do have the cover, all you have to do is to pass the solicitor's letter on to the insurance company, and they will see to the rest. But without the insurance, you could have quite a problem.

However, this is not the main reason why most people take out contents insurance. Many people invest a high proportion of their income in furnishing a house and when you include personal possessions and valuables, it is not difficult to come up with a high value. An average three-bedroom semi-detached house can easily contain £20,000-worth of contents at current replacement costs.

A basic contents policy will insure your contents against loss or damage caused by certain specified 'perils'. The list will include events such as theft, fire, explosion and water damage (e.g. water escaping from a burst pipe). Although when you look at your policy you will think this is an impressive list, do bear in mind it does not include everything. There are certain limitations in the cover.

If you really do want to be covered for most eventualities, and you don't mind paying a higher premium, you can include accidental damage.

Example

You decide you can make do with the basic 'perils' cover, as all you're really concerned about is insurance for fire, theft and burst pipes. You then decide to decorate the house but manage to kick over a pot of paint that does irreparable damage to one of your carpets. Can you claim? No, you can't, because this would only be covered if you had paid the extra to include accidental damage. Because spilling a pot of paint is not a specified 'peril' in the policy the insurance company will not pay.

It's not that the insurance company is being unfair in the above example; they're just going along with what the policy says. So don't assume you are covered for 'everything' but make sure you understand what you are buying before handing over your premium.

Even if you decide on the more basic policy for your general contents, you can still select an enhanced cover for valuables, especially those you occasionally take out and about with you. For example, you might want cover for specific items that are especially valuable, or you might be happy with a general 'all risks' cover for all your personal effects. This would enable you to claim for lost or broken cameras or for spectacles you accidentally left on the settee before you sat down!

Most contents insurances are arranged on a 'new for old' basis, so that any claim is based on the full replacement cost, even for items that are far from new. Under this type of policy, you could claim for a new carpet after a fire, even though the original was wearing thin. However, deductions for wear and tear are usually made from claims for clothing, linen and pedal cycles.

If you want to economise on premiums, you can arrange a cheaper type of cover known as 'indemnity', in which case your claim is still calculated on the full replacement price but the insurance company then deduct an amount to represent wear and tear.

HOME BUILDINGS INSURANCE

This will normally only be necessary if you actually own the home or you are buying it under a mortgage to a bank or building society. Otherwise, buildings insurance will be the responsibility of the landlord (even though, depending on your agreement, he might expect you to pay the premium!).

If you have a mortgage, whoever lends you the money normally expects to arrange the buildings insurance for you. As a general rule, this means you pay over the odds for the cover you need. You will almost always save money by making your own arrangements. Banks and building societies do not normally like you doing this, and some even charge you a fee for NOT arranging your cover! But even so, check out what is available elsewhere before committing yourself to the automatic insurance that goes along with the mortgage. A telephone call to an insurance broker should tell you whether or not you can save on the premium.

When you come to consider the type of cover you want, you have the same choice as you do under a contents policy: do you want a specified 'perils' cover, or would you rather have an accidental damage policy?

Example

At long last you decide to tidy up the house, and remember that you can hide all sorts of things in the loft. While you are up there you slip and put your foot through the rafters, making a horrible mess of the ceiling. As long as you have extended the buildings policy to include accidental damage you should be able to claim – but not if you only have the basic 'perils' cover.

WHAT'S BUILDINGS AND WHAT'S CONTENTS?

It can be difficult to know what items to insure under your buildings policy, and which ones should be treated as contents. This can make quite a difference if you are trying to calculate the amount to insure for.

The general rule to follow is this: anything you would take with you when you move is contents; anything else is buildings. Although many people these days leave carpets behind when they move, you are perfectly entitled to take these with you unless you make a specific agreement with whoever is buying your house. So carpets are always treated as contents. Conversely, although fitted furniture can sometimes be taken away if this is agreed between buyer and seller, this is not normally done, and fitted furniture, including fitted kitchens and bedrooms, are always treated as part of the building.

INSURING FOR THE FULL VALUE

Whatever it is you are insuring, you must make sure you insure for the full value – otherwise, any claims payment might well be reduced.

Example
You insure your home contents for £7,500 even though you know it would cost more than this to replace everything. But you want to pay the smallest premium possible and are prepared to accept you wouldn't be paid more than £7,500 if everything was lost.

The trouble is, all insurance companies insist you insure for the full value. So if you suffered a burglary and you lost £2,000 worth of personal effects the insurance company will probably arrange to see you, and during this meeting the representative will make an assessment of the likely replacement cost of all your contents. Let's say he decides the full replacement value would be £15,000. This would mean you were 50 per cent under-insured, so you will only receive 50 per cent of your claim – £1,000 instead of the full £2,000.

RUNNING A BUSINESS FROM HOME

Always tell your buildings and contents insurers if you plan to operate a business from home. This will be especially important if this means you have to keep business stock at home. But even if you just have a personal computer and a fax machine that you use from time to time in connection with your job, you should tell the insurers – otherwise, you could have all sorts of problems. The policy will probably exclude cover on any business items unless you notify the insurance company, and there could be problems if a visitor suffered injury and he had called on you in connection with your job. If in doubt, tell the insurance company and see what they have to say.

It can, in fact, be easy to arrange extra cover for the business. You should bear in mind that if you are running your own business and you employ anyone, you must take out employer's liability insurance, otherwise you will be breaking the law.

INSURING YOUR HEALTH

If you cannot work because of illness, there are certain state benefits you should be entitled to claim. But the chances are these are not going to be sufficient, especially if you suffer a long-term illness. There are a number of ways you can insure yourself for illness.

Permanent health insurance (PHI)

This can be quite expensive, but the policy provides a monthly benefit if you cannot work following accident or sickness. At the outset, you choose the period of cover, usually through to age sixty or sixty-five. If you are unable to work for a long period, the monthly payments will simply continue until you resume work or when you reach the 'retirement' age selected. Under this type of policy it is possible to make a number of shorter claims during your working life; even if the insurance company decide you are no longer a good risk, they are not able to cancel the policy – just so long as you continue to pay the premiums.

Personal accident and sickness

A personal accident and sickness policy is cheaper than PHI, but it is not possible to claim for such a long period. This type of policy will normally only pay for up to two years, and if you claim too often the insurance company can refuse to renew the cover! But it does represent good value, and is worth considering as an alternative to PHI.

Critical illness
This is a fairly new type of cover and is designed to pay out a lump sum benefit if you are diagnosed as having one of the 'critical illnesses' listed in the policy, such as cancer or Parkinson's disease.

Loan protection
If you take out a loan or use a credit card, you will usually be offered an insurance that should make your loan repayments for you if you are off work because of illness or redundancy. This type of insurance is extremely expensive, and usually only makes the repayments for you over a one- or two-year period. There are usually lots of exclusions and exceptions and this type of cover is not always good value for money.

Loan protection insurance is often promoted quite heavily by loan companies' sales personnel because they receive substantial commissions for a successful sale.

Because of the confusing array of sickness and redundancy covers available you should seek independent advice before committing yourself. A broker will be able to assess your need for such cover and recommend the cover best suited to your circumstances.

LIFE INSURANCE

People are often reluctant to do anything about taking out adequate life insurance for themselves. This is sometimes because life insurance has, historically, been a high-pressure business. People have hesitated to ask for advice in case they ended up being pressured into buying something they didn't really want.

One misconception is that life insurance is expensive. The

reason people think this is that, in the past, insurance companies have so often packaged life insurance schemes with all sorts of investment products. There is nothing wrong with some of these arrangements, but if all you really want to achieve is some security for your family in the event of an early death, then ordinary life insurance, without the investment or savings element, is perfectly sufficient. Have a look at the following example:

Andy is twenty-seven, and Julie is twenty-five. They could take out a joint-life temporary 'term insurance' over a twenty-five-year period for £50,000. This would cost about £15 per month.

As an alternative to term insurance, they could take out a family income benefit policy. For the same premium they could insure for a tax-free income of £5,000 p.a. over twenty-five years. This provides a good level of cover in the early years while the family is growing up and, effectively, gives an initial cover of £125,000.

Neither policy would pay anything if they both survived the twenty-five years – but if Andy and Julie want to provide a nest egg for the future, that can be dealt with a little later in life or at any time when their finances permit them to start saving on a regular basis.

How much should you insure yourself for? It is very easy to become grossly under-insured. Using the above example, assume Andy and Julie have two children and that the couple have decided that they can afford for Julie to stay at home to look after the children. This means that it is only Andy who is earning a salary. He will want to take out sufficient insurance to enable Julie to maintain a similar standard of living for herself and the children in the event of his death. Assume Andy insured his life for £100,000. He would want Julie to be able to invest this and use the interest to replace his lost income – but at current interest rates this would produce an annual gross income of only about £6,500 which probably won't be enough. So don't be put off by large figures.

11
TAXATION

'But in this world nothing can be said to be certain, except death and taxes.'

Benjamin Franklin

WHY TAXATION?

Why do we have taxation? The obvious reason is to raise money for the government, national or local, to spend. Once this is accepted, there are two other reasons for the way we are taxed. First, the political parties in this country have different ideologies about who should contribute most to the Exchequer. Should those who are paid most pay at a higher rate than those on average income? Should families be able to pass the savings of one generation down to the next? These and questions like them give rise to political decisions that have nothing to do with the business of raising money for the government to spend.

In addition the nation's social conscience has a part to play. It is true that because of the addictive nature of smoking cigarettes, the government is guaranteed a large income from any tax on tobacco. However, the loading of the tax on to forms of smoking with the highest health risk is an attempt to encourage smokers to transfer to a form of the habit a little less likely to cause disease – for which the government has to pay to provide treatment. Similarly loading tax on to leaded fuel, making unleaded fuel cheaper, is another social rather than money-raising decision.

DIFFERENT TYPES OF TAXATION

There are two types of taxation – direct and indirect. Direct taxation is the sort we are all too aware of – income tax, National Insurance contributions, capital gains tax, etc. It is the sort of tax that each individual pays because of his own income. Indirect taxation, however, is paid by the rich and poor alike. Indirect taxes include those like excise duties, value added tax and insurance premium tax.

Indirect taxation

Let us look at value added tax (VAT) as an example of indirect taxation. Currently there are three rates of VAT. Zero per cent is applied to books and food, among other things (although restaurants, whether they are providing cordon bleu cookery or are simply burger bars, all have to add VAT to their sales). A reduced rate is added to domestic gas and electricity fuel bills, and the full rate is added to most other things. Certain transactions, such as the payment of interest or the selling of postage stamps, are exempt from VAT.

Most people do not realise how much indirect tax they pay – for example, VAT and excise duties together make up some 40 per cent of the cost of a pint of beer or a bottle of wine.

Council Tax

Council Tax is a method of raising income for local government. Contrary to most people's belief, the majority of the money for local services actually comes from central government. Nonetheless, local councils do raise money from their communities. Some years ago this was based on the rateable value of property (as business rates still are). This meant that the larger the house you owned (or rented, as landlords tend to pass on local taxes to their tenants) the more you paid. This was considered to be inequitable: for instance, one old lady living in a big old house made considerably less use of local services than a young couple with two or more children attending school, living in a small council house. An alternative was put forward, entitled the Community Charge. This was a charge based on each individual living in a community or local authority area.

One could be forgiven for thinking that this was eminently more equitable as it was a charge on the individuals who were actually using the services provided by the local authority, particularly when financial help was on offer to those who could not afford to pay their share. The introduction of the charge was handled badly by the government, and a number of extreme groups began to whip up public support against this tax. There were riots in the street, more reminiscent of the imposition of the Poll Tax in earlier centuries, and the government was forced to drop the scheme. There now exists the Council Tax, which is at least honest in that it is called a tax! In fact it is an attempt to combine the old rating system with a charge based on numbers of individuals. Like many compromises, it has little basis in logic at all.

The Council Tax paid by a householder (owner or tenant) depends on the value of the property. Instead of a specific rateable value for the property, as in the old rating system, properties are now divided into 'bands'. The rate of tax assumes that two adults are living in the house; if there is only one, then a reduction is available. It takes no account of children, nor households with more adults. Although the bands of values are consistent across the country, the amount of charge is left with the individual council. The government does have some control in an indirect way, in that it can control spending by a local authority, and the individual has the opportunity to change the council at the local ballot box.

Income tax
Income tax, not surprisingly, is a tax on income. It is payable on all forms of income – wages and salaries, rents

received, interest from banks and building societies, dividends from companies and profits generated by sole traders and partnerships. It is also charged on payments made by employers to their employees for expenses, where the amount received is more than the expense incurred. There is also a whole range of payments which are taxable under income tax on employees. These 'benefits-in-kind' include the provision of a company car, payment of medical insurance by employers, low-interest loans and many more.

At the moment people earning below a certain figure pay no income tax. There is then a low rate for a small sum of taxable income before the basic rate comes into play. If you earn over a certain figure you will be taxed at higher rates.

NATIONAL INSURANCE

In addition to the tax on income, a further tax is levied on earnings. This is called National Insurance and employees, employers and the self-employed all make contributions. At one time people actually believed that they were paying into a fund which would pay their medical bills and would be invested to provide them with a pension on retirement, but this is simply not the case. The National Insurance contributions made today are used to pay the pensions of today's retired and old people.

Unfortunately for today's workers, the average age of the population is increasing. People are living longer, and advances in medical science, although verging on the miraculous, are not making treatment any cheaper. The problem facing the government of this country and others, in Europe and elsewhere, is how they will fund the pensions of those who retire in fifteen, twenty-five and more years from now. If the system remains as it is, the working population in years to come will find an ever-increasing proportion of their income being used to fund the pensions of an ever-increasing elderly population. Anybody who has the opportunity to help provide for their own future through a personal pension scheme would be well advised to do so – but that is a subject to be found elsewhere in this book (see chapter 9).

National Insurance is often seen as a hidden tax, as in the past it has not been so significant. However, with many people now only paying the lower rate of income tax an additional charge of 10 per cent is taking on more significance.

National Insurance contributions
National Insurance contributions are divided into different classes.

Class 1 (employees and employers)
Below a certain figure employees and employers pay nothing. Above that there is a sliding scale for both to pay.

Class 2 (self-employed)
This is a flat-rate contribution that all self-employed people must pay. Benefits will be lost if this is not the case. If earnings are really low you can get a certificate to exempt paying the stamp, but this still could have a negative impact on any future benefit claims.

Class 4 (self-employed)
A percentage of profits is paid between a minimum and maximum figure.

HOW IS INCOME TAX ON WAGES AND SALARIES COLLECTED?

Income tax and National Insurance contributions on wages and salaries are collected through the Pay As You Earn (PAYE) system. This can be one of the simplest, most efficient and painless ways of dealing with the Inland Revenue. On the other hand, it can be one of the most frustrating and infuriating systems. The heart of the system is a code number issued to every employee and their employer. The employee is sent a detailed form showing how the code number has been calculated and the employer receives a notification of the number alone, thus preserving the employee's privacy.

How is your code number calculated? The left-hand side of the notice is where your allowances are shown. Everyone has a personal allowance and married couples have an additional allowance. This is usually given to the husband unless husband and wife have told the Revenue they would like it dealt with differently. If you pay professional subscriptions which are allowable against tax, then these will also be shown on the left-hand side, as well as certain mortgage or other allowable interest. The amounts are totalled and the amount for total allowances is shown.

The right-hand column lists the items which are to be deducted from the allowances. The deductions will include an amount for any car provided by your employer, and the fuel benefit as well if your employer does not charge you for privately used petrol or diesel. Any other benefits in kind are included – these may range from private health premiums to mobile phone usage. Also included on this side is any income which is taxable, where income tax is not deducted at source. The most obvious example is the state pension or other taxable state benefits.

Your PAYE code is the difference between the left-hand side (allowances) and the right-hand side (restrictions), divided by 10. If the subtraction produces a negative figure, then the code is preceded by a letter K. Your employer will increase your taxable salary by the amount shown in his code book, rather than reducing it, before working out your tax liability. The other letters used after the number are merely to help employers introduce Budget changes to allowances without the need to reissue all the code notices.

Pay As You Earn works by giving you one-twelfth of your allowances each month, on a cumulative basis. Thus if a mistake was made when your code number was prepared, the first month the correct code number is used you will automatically receive a tax repayment for all the months the wrong number was used. If the change in your code number would bring about a large deduction for an amount owing to the Revenue, then usually the code number will be used on a 'Month 1' basis. This means that each month the code is used, it is treated as being the first month of the tax year, and the code number does not operate on a cumulative basis.

HOW IS INCOME TAX ON INCOME FROM SAVINGS COLLECTED?

Income tax on interest from banks and building societies as well as companies paying dividends is charged at a flat rate. Normally this is collected by the bank or building society when they pay interest net of tax. They then pay over all the tax to the Revenue. This saves a huge amount of work for the Revenue, and for millions of individuals who would otherwise be responsible for making the payment themselves.

If your total income (before deduction of income tax) does not exceed the allowances to which you are entitled, you can complete a form (available from banks and building societies) which will enable them to pay you your interest without deducting income tax at source.

SELF ASSESSMENT

If it is not collected through the PAYE system or by deduction at source, how is income tax, and indeed other taxes, calculated and collected? From 5 April 1997 a new system was introduced. In the past, taxpayers who were sent a tax return had to fill in all their income details and allowance claims and submit the form to the Inland Revenue for them to issue assessments, but now the taxpayer can calculate his own tax bill should he wish. Not everyone with taxable income will be sent a tax return every year – people whose income is taxed under the PAYE system will not usually be sent a form. People who are self-employed, or who have rental income or interest untaxed at source, will probably get a form every year.

It has to be stated that the notification of liability to any tax is the responsibility of the taxpayer. It is insufficient to argue that you were not sent a tax return, or that you were not sent the specific schedules relating to a source of income. You have the responsibility of asking for the forms and the correct schedules if you believe you should pay tax.

The basic tax return comprises eight pages; there are additional schedules for specific types of income. The Inland Revenue will send you the forms and schedules they think you will need, but you must ask for any others you discover you require. The form has to be completed if you are sent one. It can be returned to the Tax Office by 30 September and the Inland Revenue staff will calculate the tax that is due and let you know in good time before 31 January the following year. If you fail to make the deadline, or wish to calculate your own liability, the return does not have to be sent back until 31 January.

On 31 January, you are required to make a payment on account of half your liability for the year; the other half is due on 31 July. It may be that these payments are estimates, or wrong for some other reason. If this is the case, then any balance of tax owed has to be sent with the first instalment of the following year on the next 31 January. Interest will be charged on late payment of income tax. Each month throughout the year you will receive a statement showing the current position on your account with the Inland Revenue.

The tax return and schedules list all forms of income and require you to complete specific boxes with the details. There is then a calculation sheet should you wish (or have) to calculate your own liability. The totals from various pages in the return are transferred to the working sheet, and then additions and subtractions and multiplications take place until your liability is finally calculated. You will require a calculator, and must be able to follow instructions without giving any thought as to what they mean. In trials, accountants and tax advisers have made all sorts of mistakes because they tried to follow their understanding of the law rather than simply do what they were told to do!

If you have suffered deduction of tax at source, or even under the PAYE system, and your liability is less than the tax you have paid, then you will be sent a refund. Where the refund is delayed, you will be entitled to a repayment supplement (in other words, interest!).

CAPITAL GAINS TAX

Another tax that you may come across is capital gains tax. This is a tax on any transaction involving almost everything you own! To be more precise, if you sell an antique piece of furniture, for example, you will have to pay tax on the profit you make, and likewise if you sell shares in a quoted company. The profit is calculated as being the difference between the amount you paid for the object, or its value at 31 March 1982, and the amount you sell it for. There is also an addition to the cost which is known as indexation. This seeks to take account of inflation since 1982. The indexation amount is based on Revenue-calculated factors. There is no tax, however, on gains on 'chattels' – furniture, paintings, etc. – if the sale price is below a certain figure. Likewise, there is no capital gains tax on your own home, nor on motor cars. When the gain is made on retirement, very generous reliefs are available to reduce gains made on assets used in a business or in agriculture.

Capital gains tax is due even if you give the asset away rather than sell it. In this case the market value replaces the sale price. Indeed, if the object is lost or stolen or destroyed by fire, and you make a claim on your insurance, then capital gains tax could be charged. By the way, do not think you can avoid the tax by selling the asset at a reduced value to a friend or relative. Again, market value is used instead of the selling price. The only exception to this rule is that transfers – gifts or sales – between husband and wife are free of all capital gains tax. This is a very useful point, as we shall see.

If, when the calculations are completed, you have actually made a loss rather than a profit, then you can use that loss against any other gains you make in the future until the whole of the loss is used up. Finally, when the gain is calculated after indexation, and after any losses made in the same tax year or brought forward from earlier years, it is only the amount of net gain over the figure applying at that time which is taxable. This chargeable gain is entered on the tax return and is included in the same way as income, and therefore taxed at the applicable rate.

INHERITANCE TAX

The final word on taxation is inheritance tax. This tax is charged on gifts made throughout a person's lifetime, and on the amount of the estate on death. There are some reliefs: small gifts to any one person in a year and gifts up to a certain figure in any tax year are exempt. If you do not make gifts one year then the relief is carried forward, but for one year only. There is also an allowance for regular gifts which are made out of income and do not affect the giver's standard of living. Close relatives can also give a happy couple gifts at the time of their wedding without incurring a tax charge. There is no inheritance tax on gifts between partners in a marriage. Finally, all gifts to charities and political parties, whether during life or on death, are generally exempt from inheritance tax.

Inheritance tax is charged at nil up to a certain amount

and above that at a fixed rate. Gifts that are chargeable and are made during your lifetime are taxed at half these rates. Gifts during the seven years prior to death are accumulated with the estate and charged at the death rates, although there is some tapering relief available to reduce the charge. Business and agricultural assets are left out of the account, but your home is not!

It is vital that everyone prepares a will as soon as they have any independence. It is very easy to be wealthy on death, even at a young age. There can be insurance policies or travel policies which suddenly come into the calculations. Without a will, the property that is left is apportioned under the rules of intestacy. This may well not be the way you would like your belongings to go. An obvious example is that of a young engaged couple – without a will the remaining fiancé or fiancée would receive nothing at all. The deceased may not have intended this.

It is also important to remember that a will becomes invalid as soon as the testator marries. The only exception to this is if the will is clearly written to be valid after the marriage to a specific named person.

Blank will forms can be obtained from reputable stationers. As long as your affairs are simple, such a form and the explanations that accompany it are usually quite sufficient. If your affairs are more complex, then having a will drawn up by a solicitor need not be very expensive.

CHARITABLE GIVING

Since taxation has considerable implications for charitable giving, this section takes a second look at the information introduced in chapter 8.

As has been stated, there is no inheritance tax on gifts made to registered charities. Likewise, there is no capital gains tax on gifts to charities. It is better, therefore, to make a gift of quoted company shares to a charity rather than sell them yourself (incurring a possible charge to capital gains tax) and give the money to charity. Even if the charity sells the shares immediately, it is exempt from paying capital gains tax.

Normally, however, an individual would like to make a smaller donation to charity. There are tax reliefs available to encourage such action. First, a taxpayer may enter into a deed of covenant with a charity. To be effective for tax purposes, such a deed must be capable of being in force for more than three years. For this reason they are often referred to as four-year deeds, although they could be of any longer length. I have heard of one charity that impressed its prospective donors by telling them it would receive almost twice as much if only they would make their deeds for seven years. This is hardly surprising as seven years is almost twice the minimum four-year period!

A deed of covenant is a legal document, but one of the few that does not need to be drawn up by a solicitor. The donor agrees to make a regular payment to the charity (of any amount), and the charity is then able to treat the receipt as net of income tax and reclaim the income tax from the Inland Revenue. The donor must have a gross taxable income (after allowances, but before any deduction of income tax) at least equal to the amount of the grossed up covenanted payment. If this is not the case, the Inland Revenue will ask the donor to pay the income tax reclaimed by the charity. It is important to note that the deed must be completed and signed before the first gift is made for it to be valid for income tax purposes.

Single amounts over a certain sum can be given to a charity under the Gift Aid scheme. They can give rise to a reclaim of income tax by the charity in the same way as a payment under a deed of covenant, and the same restriction on the donor applies. Gifts can be made, however, without any forms being signed first. Indeed, the charity will probably send a Gift Aid form for completion to any donor generous enough to send a cheque for that amount or more.

Where an individual would like to make a single payment to a specific charity but the amount is less than can be used for Gift Aid, it can be arranged as a Loan Covenant or Deposit Covenant. Here, again, the paperwork has to be completed in advance of the making of the gift. The donor enters into a simple agreement to deposit with the charity, on Day One, a sum sufficient to cover the four annual payments under a deed of covenant. For example, a gift of £100 would be treated as four payments of £25 under a deed of covenant.

Should an individual wish to be flexible in the charities he supports and in the amounts he gives in any year, then it is possible to use an agency. Such an agency is the Charities Aid Foundation (although there are many others, and the charities you would like to help may be happy to recommend an alternative). In this case, the deed of covenant is made with the agency, which reclaims the tax, and the donor can give away gross sums in a similar way to operating a bank account.

Finally, some employers are happy to operate a Give As You Earn scheme, where an amount is deducted from the employee's gross salary (before it is taxed). These funds are then available to be distributed as the employee wishes. There is a limit to how much can be given each year under this scheme.

TAX-SAVING HINTS

Every man has the right to legally reduce the tax burden he has to shoulder. This is where the distinction between tax avoidance and tax evasion is important. The former is legal and the latter definitely is not! A few points worth noting for married couples are listed below:

- Always check your tax forms. As soon as you receive either a notice of coding or a notice of assessment, make sure your tax inspector has worked things out correctly. If not, you have only thirty days to appeal against a notice of assessment.

Financial Tips for the Family

- Don't delay in sending back your completed tax return. It should be returned by 31 January of the following year if you want to avoid an automatic penalty of £100.

- Keep your records well organised – not only is this now a legal requirement but it could also help you pay less tax. Remember the expenses you can offset against your tax bill. Some examples of these would be:

  What you spend on meals and accommodation while temporarily working away from home.

  Incidental expenses, e.g. newspapers, phone calls, laundry, when temporarily away from home whether in the UK or overseas.

  The cost of travel between two places of work for the same employer.

  A proportion of car expenses.

  Subscriptions.

  Cost of maintaining and replacing tools, etc., necessary for your job.

  A percentage of heating, lighting, cleaning, etc., if working from home.

  Any special clothing/uniforms you need for your job.

  Specialist reference books.

  Some training fees.

  Interest on loans which you need to buy capital equipment.

- If self-employed you can normally claim:

  Cost of goods you use or sell.

  Selling costs such as advertising.

  Office or factory expenses such as heating, lighting, etc.

  Cost of computer software, if purchased separately from hardware.

  Proportion of home expenses if used for work.

Professional magazines, etc., needed for your business.

Travel expenses (but not normally between home and work) and running costs of car, etc.

Accountancy and audit fees.

Staff expenses.

Cost of employing your married partner.

Staff entertainment.

Bank charges on business account.

Interest on loans and overdrafts for business purposes.

The interest element of hire purchase payments.

Business insurance.

Specific bad debts.

Many legal charges.

Premium for leases.

- Where one married partner has a low income and can't use up all their allowances they should consider transferring them to the other partner. The most common would be the married couple's allowance.

- If one of you pays tax at the higher rate consider reorganising your investments so that the income on these is paid to the other partner, who will pay less tax on it.

- There is a range of fringe benefits which are tax-free whatever your earnings level. These include:
    Luncheon vouchers up to a certain level per day.
    Contributions to an approved or statutory pension scheme.
    Meal, where provided for all employees on the employer's premises.
    Up to a certain level for reasonable relocation expenses.
    Christmas parties.

Medical insurance for treatment needed while abroad with your job.

Medical check-ups.

The cost of a group insurance policy.

Professional indemnity insurance to cover your liability at work.

The provision of childcare facilities by your employer.

Cheap or interest-free loans up to a certain level.

Subscriptions paid to professional bodies, if approved by the Inland Revenue.

Goods and services your employer lets you have at cost to them.

Essential books and fees.

The cost of taxis if you have been working late and public transport has ended (or it would be unreasonable to ask you to use it).

Car parking near your work.

In-house sports facilities.

- If you have a company car try and use it for at least 2,500 miles a year for business purposes as it can cut your tax bill on your car by a third. If you do heavy business mileage try and get it above 18,000 miles, as this will halve your tax bill. You will need to keep very good records of your business mileage to substantiate these claims.

- If you run your own business consider employing your spouse if they do not work elsewhere. It could save money if you pay your spouse first under the lower earnings limit for National Insurance contributions.

- Consider leasing cars rather than buying outright. VAT can be reclaimed on leasing payments but not on the cost of a purchased car.

- Remember, a married couple can choose to share the tax relief on mortgage interest however they like. If some split other than an equal one would save you tax, make an 'allocation of interest' election.

- If you have a home improvement loan taken out before 6 April 1988 consider carefully before you replace it with another loan even if it has a lower rate of interest. You will not be able to claim tax relief on the interest paid on the replacement loan.

- If you let out a room in your house under the rent-a-room scheme you can take up to a certain sum of gross rent tax-free.

- Non-taxpayers investing in things like banks and building societies where basic-rate tax is deducted from the income should ensure they are claiming it back from the Inland Revenue. Interest can in fact be paid gross to non-taxpayers.

- Do not forget to claim losses if you dispose of something like shares or valuables at a loss. Losses can be offset against taxable gains and carried over to later years.

12
YOUR CHILDREN AND MONEY

One of the greatest things you can do for your children is to help them learn to handle money sensibly. I believe that they can be taught simply from a very young age; as they grow older so the teaching can become more detailed. To begin with you could do a lot worse than use a money-box. Every week you can give your child a small sum of money which is put into the box. Your child can then spend the money as needs and wants arise, but when the box is empty the spending has to stop. Do not give in to heartfelt pleas for an advance!

This method will quickly demonstrate a basic but profound rule of handling money. The money-box is not a bottomless pit and therefore spending has to be restricted to what it actually contains. By its very nature this system means that debt cannot occur and your children learn to spend only what they have.

Another way of teaching your children is to use the envelope system. You give them a number of envelopes with labels on the outside indicating what the money in that particular envelope is to be used for. The various envelopes can be kept in a box and the same rules apply as for a money-box, so again your children learn not to commit money they haven't actually got.

These two systems demonstrate, in very basic format, the two key points of any budget. First, there needs to be a plan for spending and, second, there must be a system of controls to ensure that the spending is never greater than the plan allows. This is vital for our children to learn in today's society, because the over-use of credit allows us to live on a day-by-day basis, as if there really is no bottom to our money-box and therefore no limit to our spending. Eventually sources of finance, even to extra credit, will dry up and this will almost certainly be at a time when a lifestyle has been established that will make it impossible to start repaying. As this pressure can lead to divorce or bankruptcy or both, you can see that teaching your children the sensible use of money early on could save them enormous heartache later. **People who struggle with money do not plan to fail, they simply fail to plan!**

The system that you decide to adopt will depend on your preferences as well as the ages of your children. As an example, let me demonstrate one simple system that can be used effectively by children as young as seven – the envelope system mentioned earlier.

A young child could have envelopes with 'saving', 'spending' and 'gifts' on them. The 'spending' envelope will have money in it that can be used in any way the child wants. The 'gifts' envelope is the amount set aside to be used in buying presents, etc., at Christmas, birthdays and other special occasions for relatives and friends. Every month the children are given an allowance in cash to put in the envelopes according to a pre-set plan. This is after an annual discussion between parents and children has agreed the relevant figure required each year which is then divided into twelve so that they receive the same lump sum every month. During the year the children can also either 'earn' extra money by doing various jobs around the house or receive gift money from other relatives. To begin with, the children are encouraged to put 10 per cent into both the 'giving' and 'saving' envelopes, but as they grow older and understand the point of the system they are given the freedom to put money where they want to. Alongside this system, of course, children need to be helped and to see the benefits and value of giving and saving. That way, as they start choosing for themselves, they will enjoy making the decisions because they have experienced the benefits of them.

As they grow older further envelopes can be added to this system. So, for example, if you decided you would be paying for all your children's clothes until the age of eleven you would wait until your children were that age and then give them another envelope with the word 'clothes' on it. At the same time you would increase their allowance to ensure that they had enough to buy the clothes they need (not necessarily those they want). Children need to learn by their mistakes at home, and they will make them. So do not constantly bail them out when they run out of money. Life is not like that.

Expect your children to make mistakes. If they do so regularly, such as spending money on designer jeans and then having no money left over for shoes, there are several ways of dealing with the problem. First, you may decide they are not yet mature enough to deal with the 'necessities' such as clothes for school. So you reduce their allowance and buy those things for them. Second, you could simply let them go without. Third, you can let them live with the consequences of having to wear last year's coat, shoes or whatever: having to wear last year's shoes with holes in them during the winter months would certainly provide a short sharp shock. Last, you can encourage them to earn the extra money needed for the purchase. Whatever method you choose, the point is that children should have responsibility for certain budget items and they have to learn to allocate properly within the various categories.

For bigger purchases, such as a bicycle, children will have to be saving for some considerable time. But when they have got enough they can simply take the envelope with them and use the cash in it to make the purchase. The amount for each category will vary for each child because of age and the various activities they participate in. A child who is very keen on sport or music, for example, may need some extra incentive to enable him to continue in these areas – especially where extra tuition can prove expensive.

As children get older, parents will need to make decisions based on their own wishes and circumstances as to whether their child should take paid work outside the home. For example, if your son is good at football and plays a lot during the season you may require him not to work at that time. But during the summer months, when he has time on his hands, you may well want to encourage him to get a job.

How frequently to give the allowance really depends on the age of the children. If you begin the system with very young children it probably should be given weekly because a month is too long a period for them to grasp. However, by the time they have reached nine or ten they could be given their money on a monthly basis. So, for example, their clothes allowance for the year would be divided by twelve and given to them monthly. They then have the responsibility for the money in the envelopes, the freedom of decision-making and the likelihood of failing – but in a safe environment.

Many parents will no doubt be concerned that their children will spend unwisely if they receive a large amount on a monthly basis. This in fact may well be true in the beginning, but it is precisely through a series of mistakes that they will learn to plan more wisely. It is vital that they have the freedom to make their own decisions and learn by their own mistakes.

Once you have decided on an amount for each category and you are happy that the figure agreed is fair, do not be persuaded to change it without giving it serious thought. It is very easy to be manipulated by your children!

If they learn that they can constantly increase the amount given to them by arguing, sulking or even just asking, the whole point of learning about spending a finite amount has been destroyed. The world is doing all it can to convince us and our children that we can have all we want NOW – no matter what the cost will be in the future. It is already an incredibly difficult job trying to teach children to wait until they can afford things before buying them. Giving in and allowing them unlimited resources will only add to their problems.

On the other hand, do not be so rigid as to make your children rebel. You are not training them to be chartered accountants, and therefore they should not be required to keep track of every penny they spend from each envelope. If children want to know why they are running out of money each month in a particular envelope and therefore want to keep track of how they are spending it, that's fine, but they should not be required to do so automatically.

I believe strongly that the regular allowance should not be withheld as punishment or to influence behaviour. Nor should it be changed depending on the amount of work the child does around the home. There are other ways to motivate children – and giving extra for good behaviour is much more sensible than taking away money that they need. Similarly with jobs around the home. As children get older they should be expected to do more – such as making their bed and keeping their room tidy. Other jobs can be optional. So if your child volunteers to baby-sit, wash the car or cut the grass (i.e. any job that either parent would normally do), you may well feel inclined to give them extra for doing so.

Whatever you do, try and be flexible – encourage your children to think of it as their system. Help them set up and understand how it works, but then give them the freedom to adapt it to best suit their individual needs.

In summary, therefore, you need to do the following:

1 Discuss the system with your children, making sure they understand the extent of their responsibility.
2 Review the amounts required and then set allowances for each of your children.
3 Give your children the envelopes with the correct amount of money in each of the envelopes for the first month. Always pay the agreed amount in full on the agreed day, every month.

4 Be prepared to be flexible without constantly giving in to demands for more.
5 Be encouraged as you watch your children take increasing responsibility in this very important area of their lives.

What the system teaches
Although the envelope scheme is by no means the only one you could use, we have found that it helps teach children many things. These include:

Reward for work
By having a limited supply of money children must earn additional money for any discretionary items they want. So when they then make a purchase they are learning the significant reward for work.

Saving
Saving teaches the principle of delayed gratification. Putting money into a 'savings' envelope on a regular basis establishes a discipline that should ensure financial success. Allowing some of the savings to be spent periodically for significant items will begin to teach the benefits of delaying acquiring things.

The cost of consumption
When the money has gone there is no money left to spend on anything else. There is no more dramatic way of teaching this than going to the envelope and finding it is empty.

Limited supply of money
The whole system is built around the principle that there is a limited amount of money. When the envelope is empty the only way to get more money is to do extra work. Despite what society tries to tell us, there really is a limit to how much we can spend.

Decision-making
Dealing with a limited resource and an unlimited number of choices on how to spend these resources means that careful decisions have to be made.

Budgeting
Budgeting teaches how to plan and balance income and expenditure – something your children will find very useful for the rest of their lives.

Spending with care
Over time children learn that by buying wisely they will have more money left over for other things.

Setting goals
As your children get older they may well set longer and longer goals. They may even, in time, be able to save up enough to buy something as expensive as a computer. Obviously, for an item such as this it would be better to save through some form of interest-bearing account. Think how cherished and well looked after those items will be when they have been saved up for and finally purchased for cash!

The problems of peer pressure
Peer pressure, particularly in the teenage years, can be a real problem but I believe the envelope system actually helps overcome this. Rather than buying clothes for your children you are giving them the choice of spending their money on their clothes in any way they desire. Obviously with a limited amount of money there are restrictions on what they can buy. They will usually end up with a choice, either a variety of clothes which they feel happy with or just a few 'designer-label' items which will have to be worn very regularly.

Peer pressure is not, at the end of the day, a money issue. It is to do with self-worth. The envelope system encourages the child to buy what they feel good in and thus adds to their self-worth. If they desire more clothes that are above and beyond their budget the answer is simple – they can work for what they want. They will very quickly discover whether their acceptance by their peer group is as important as the time required to work for what this peer group says they should have. This incidentally is exactly the same problem we as parents face when we are tempted to 'keep up with the Joneses'.

Preparing for college or university

In the last few years the government has cut grants to people going to college, with the result that more and more students are having to borrow significant sums of money to keep them through their time there.

How you fund college education is realistically limited to a few alternatives. These include:

- Pay as you go along by taking money out of your existing earnings.

- Plan ahead by using a savings scheme that matures at the time your child is ready to go to college.

- Insist that your child takes advantage of bank interest-free overdrafts and student loans to top up a grant.

- Tell your child that they must work to make up the shortfall.

- A combination of some or all of the above.

There is no right way to fund university education. The most sensible way, where possible, is to begin saving early so that when the children reach college age the money is already there. Obviously to do this you are going to have to sacrifice significant spending in the previous years unless you are on a very high salary. Whatever your decision, it is important that you make your decision as quickly as you can so you can relay it to your children. This will mean that they will not then be living with false illusions.

Even if you do decide you can afford to help with a significant amount of their expenses, do not spoil them by letting them constantly have more. Instead, give them the opportunity to manage money by giving them a lump sum, either annually or at the beginning of each term.

Emergencies

Even when your children have eventually 'flown the nest' you may still want to step in at times of real emergency. This could include marital breakdown, loss of job or the special needs of a handicapped child, for example. I always believe that in genuine cases like this it is better to give rather than loan because the very act of lending tends to change the parent–child relationship. Equally it does your children no favours at all to lend money to them so they can buy things that are non-essential. Years of working with your children on money matters should mean that their expectation and the reality of the situation are the same. It is only when expectation is different from the reality of the situation that there will be conflict, and this again shows why it is so necessary to communicate with your children over what is happening financially, at all times and at the earliest possible opportunities.

13
SAVING ON FOOD

British supermarkets make four times as much profit on a customer's weekly shopping basket as stores in the rest of Europe or in America. This is despite frequent claims of price wars, and this means that one has to be extremely careful when buying food. Like housing, food is an essential part of every budget and normally accounts for nearly 15 per cent of the net disposable income of an average family. Because certain items are promoted as 'loss leaders' other products can have a mark-up as high as 100 per cent and it is therefore vital to shop sensibly. Food is a very important area when it comes to saving money as it is probably the most flexible part of any budget. When over-spending takes place elsewhere it is usually spending on food which is cut back first.

Stores tend to reduce the price of high-profile items such as bread and milk and use these in advertisements to entice customers. However, the price of other items in the weekly shop can be artificially high. The average profit per item works out at around 6.6 per cent – compare that with the figure of 1.7 per cent per item which appears to be uniform in the United States, Germany and France. One survey found that one major UK supermarket's average basket of goods actually had a return of 8.7 per cent – fourteen times more than the cheapest supermarket in Germany. This explains why the profit margins of all five leading British supermarkets (Sainsbury, Safeway, Tesco, Asda and Morrisons) have increased dramatically over the last decade. Robert Clarke, director of the research company Corporate

Intelligence on Retailing, believes that the supermarkets are not even trying to reduce prices. And Professor Jim Lang, of the Centre for Food Study at Thames Valley University, believes that 'consumers are increasingly going to see themselves as captive and to see the disadvantages of allowing these over-powerful companies to dominate our daily food'.

Given the above, it is essential that we play the supermarkets at their own game. We need to be disciplined, buying only what we really need at prices we can really afford. It is also worth remembering that, as a general rule, the bigger the supermarket and the wider the choice of products on offer the bigger will be the 'mark-up' and the greater the temptation to stray from your shopping list!

To maximise savings on food shopping a detailed plan of action needs to be put into place even before you put your foot out of your front door. It is important to think of ways of cutting back your spending on food prior to drawing up your shopping list. Consider whether by making some minor adjustments to your usual routine you could make significant savings. For example:

- Is anyone in your family regularly eating out at lunchtime or buying sandwiches? Packed lunches work out much cheaper. Even a Thermos flask will soon pay for itself if coffee, tea, etc., has to be paid for at work.

- Is there a young baby in the family? There is usually a very high mark-up on baby foods so buying an inexpensive blender and making your own can result in tremendous savings.

- Do you like gardening? If so, do you have space that could be turned into a vegetable garden? The results should be both cheap and tasty.

- Do you enjoy cooking and do you have plenty of time to do it? If so, jams, mayonnaise, cakes, etc., can be made for a fraction of the price you pay for them in the supermarket.

BOX 1 FIVE CHEAP PASTA DISHES

Spaghetti alla carbonara Chop and fry a few rashers of streaky bacon or bacon 'misshapes'. Add to a bowl of cooked spaghetti and toss with 4 fluid ounces of single cream and 1 egg until the egg is hot but not scrambled.

Pasta arrabbiata Sauté chopped onion, garlic and bacon in a little butter. Add chopped tomato and a little chilli powder. Simmer until thick, then season and add to cooked pasta.

Pasta formaggi Make a cheese sauce using any cheese of your choice. Stir in cooked pasta.

Pepper pasta Sauté sliced red and yellow peppers in olive oil, add to cooked pasta with grated parmesan.

Pasta verde Sauté green vegetables (broccoli, courgettes and/or peas) until tender. Blend with sour cream until smooth. Toss into cooked pasta.

PLANNING YOUR MENU

Once you are satisfied that costs have been trimmed as far as possible you need to plan in detail your menu for the coming week. This needs to be looked at both nutritionally and financially to ensure that you are saving money but at the same time providing a healthy balanced diet for your family. Take into account some of the menu suggestions in this chapter when planning your weekly menu but also consider some of the other factors listed below:

- Advertisements for special price discounted foodstuffs that you would regularly buy in any event. Try to plan your menus around your supermarket's current special offers. Obviously these change from time to time so keep up to date.

- Bulk-buy discounts. ONLY buy in bulk when the items are part of your budget. There is no point in buying 'three for the price of two' if you are likely to end up using only one or if the product would be past its sell-by date before you could use all of it. Tinned items are a good buy in this category because they have a long shelf life.

- Seasonal variations. It is important to plan to take full advantage of any seasonal variations in price. The price of many fresh products fluctuates wildly during the course of the year. For example, many fruits have to be imported during the winter months so enjoy fruits and vegetables when they are in season and therefore plentiful and cheap.

- Money-off coupons. Very often available in newspapers, magazines or on products you have already purchased. If it is an item you buy regularly try and stock up when the purchase price is at its lowest. Even if it is not your usual brand it could be worth switching for a few weeks if it would mean a substantial saving.

BOX 2 FIVE CHEAP SOUPS

Soups are warming, nutritious and healthy. They are also very cheap to make, especially when using home-grown vegetables.

Parsnip soup Sauté chopped parsnips and onion in a little butter, then add chicken stock and simmer until vegetables are soft. Blend until smooth with milk and seasoning.

French onion soup Sauté sliced onion, add beef stock, a dash of any left-over wine, tomato purée and dried thyme. Simmer until the onions are tender. Serve with croutons and grated cheese.

Leek and potato soup Sauté cubed potatoes and sliced leeks in a little butter. Add chicken stock and cook until vegetables are soft. Blend until smooth with a little cream or milk. Season to taste.

Pea and ham soup Sauté chopped onion with left-over ham. Add peas and chicken stock and simmer. Blend until smooth and season.

Carrot soup Substitute carrots for parsnips in the first recipe.

At this point it is worth checking through the fridge and freezer to see what is already available. Anything near its sell-by date needs to be incorporated into the menu and used quickly, otherwise it will have to be thrown away. Look at what tinned goods you have which can be included. Planning a menu should not be over-taxing as surveys have indicated that the average British family eats only about twenty different meals.

If your family drinks a lot of milk it is worth buying large multi-pint packs from the supermarket rather than having it delivered daily by the milkman.

Also remember that:

- Junk foods are generally low in nutritional value and high in price.

- There are certain products that have a high mark-up price but little nutritional value – for example, many sugar-coated cereals fall into this category.

- When buying ready-prepared instant meals you are paying for very expensive labour.

SUPERMARKET SHOPPING

It is sensible to shop for groceries only once a week. The more we go shopping the more we are tempted to spend. Plan a detailed menu for each meal over the next seven days and once this is complete transfer the items to a written shopping list. Of course, there is little point in making a list if you don't stick to it! So the list needs to be really specific. Write down what sort of meat, which cut and how much you need. This would be equally true of items such as cartons of milk and loaves of bread. As you go round the supermarket cross off each item as you put it in the trolley.

It is also important to understand unit pricing. Put simply, this means being able to work out whether it is cheaper to buy the bigger or the smaller size, as well as calculating which brand offers the best value for money. In most cases the large economy size is the best value but you shouldn't assume that this is always the case, especially if there are 'money off' offers about. Trying to work out the best value is a good reason for taking a calculator to the supermarket. Buying large amounts is only a good idea if you are able to use all of the item before its sell-by date.

BOX 3 FIVE CHEAP RICE DISHES

Mushroom risotto Sauté sliced mushrooms and onion in butter, add risotto rice, then chicken stock in batches. When rice is tender and liquid absorbed stir in grated cheese.

Paella Sauté chopped onion and garlic, sliced red pepper, peas, cooked chicken slices with cooked rice. Add a few prawns, mussels and parsley.

Pilau Fry one onion and add pre-cooked rice, with left-over chicken meat, vegetables and curry paste; heat, stirring.

Kedgeree Boil rice with curry powder and stock. Drain, then stir in cooked, flaked smoked fish, and chopped hard-boiled egg. Keep stirring until hot.

Chinese fried rice Sauté sliced carrot, mushrooms, beansprouts and peppers in a little butter. Add five-spice powder, soy sauce and drained, cooked rice and stir-fry.

When buying short-dated food it is probably better to consider the price and size for each serving. For example, if your child has a small appetite it is better to buy four small bananas rather than two big ones which would probably be left half eaten. Always make your calculations trying to waste as little food as possible.

If at all possible (and I know it is difficult) try to avoid taking your children food shopping. On the rare occasions when I have had to take my five-year-old he seems like an octopus in a supermarket. He can reach all sorts of chocolates and biscuits and seems to know the adverts for half the products in the shop. He is more than capable of exerting pressure to get me to buy things I would not otherwise have bought and I have probably forgotten half the essential items on the list because I am so harassed and eager to get him out of the shop. I have a suspicion that it is not just my children who behave in this way! It is important to remember that much advertising is geared towards children, and if we ourselves are likely to be influenced by advertising how much greater is the influence on our children.

It is also important not to go grocery shopping when you are hungry! It is always best to shop straight after a satisfying meal. If you are hungry everything will look so tempting that you will find some 'extra' item impossible to resist. The smells and sights of the bakery section are particularly tempting. A very large percentage of bakery products purchased in supermarkets are impulse buys, so get through that area as quickly as possible.

The timing of your visit to the supermarket can also be important, especially if your menu contains many items of fresh produce. These are often marked down quite significantly at the end of the day so take advantage of this and buy items you can either use immediately or freeze for the future.

BOX 4 FIVE CHEAP POTATO DISHES

Tuna fish cakes Mix mashed potatoes with canned tuna fish, beaten egg and seasoning to taste. Press into cake-sized patties and shallow fry until golden.

Potato cheesies Substitute grated cheese and a little pickle for tuna and prepare as before.

Baked potatoes Fill with either grated cheese, baked beans or tuna fish and mayonnaise.

Spanish tortilla In a frying pan, sauté sliced potatoes and onion until tender, add beaten egg and seasoning; slowly cook until egg sets.

Meatballs Form small balls from mashed potatoes with minced meat, curry paste, spring onion and seasoning. Deep fry until golden.

Surveys have found that men tend to spend 10 per cent more on average when shopping for food and also tend to buy more expensive items. Please, men, this is not an excuse for putting your feet up and arguing that it is in the family's best interest for you never to shop again! Rather, we have to learn to be as thrifty as our partners.

It is important to remember that supermarkets, like all shops, are going to tempt you to spend your money. Very often essential items such as bread, dairy and meat products are at the back of the store and this means that you have to pass row after row of tempting goodies before you get to them. My only advice is to keep your eyes firmly on your shopping list.

Surveys also indicate that the longer you are in a supermarket the more impulse buys you are likely to make. For this reason alone, try not to hang around too long – aim to be in and out in thirty minutes. As you are thinking what to buy try not to pick up items that are not on your list as this increases the temptation to buy.

There is a greater temptation to buy luxuries at the beginning of the month when you have just been paid, but doing this could mean that you run out of essentials before the end of the month.

There is also a natural tendency to buy more when your shopping trolley is empty. That is why many items with a high profit margin are often found on the first few aisles. Another ploy is to move produce around the store. The store is hoping that when you go to the place where the baked beans used to be and there are now boxes of after-dinner mints you will end up buying both!

BOX 5 FIVE CHEAP EGG DISHES

Buck rarebit Spread toast with mustard and cheese. Grill until golden. Top with freshly poached egg and cheese sauce. Season.

Tuna and sweetcorn bake Drain can of tuna and one of sweetcorn and divide between ramekin dishes. Crack eggs on top and sprinkle over cheese. Bake until set.

Frittate Sauté sliced red peppers and onion until soft. Add beaten eggs. Cook, stirring until the eggs are set.

Florentine eggs Sauté frozen, sliced spinach. Add nutmeg and seasoning. Top each serving with a poached egg and cheese sauce.

Egg and ham on toast Top toast with sliced ham, freshly poached egg and cheese sauce. Garnish with chopped parsley to serve.

The first place to go on arriving at the supermarket is the 'reduced item' shelves (usually at the end of each aisle) to see if there are any items there that you have planned to include in your weekly menu. Also consider whether there is anything that has been reduced so substantially that it would be worth substituting it for something else on your menu. If this is the case, don't forget to cross off the original item from your shopping list before going any further.

As you are going through the store use a calculator to keep a running total of your expenditure. This soon becomes quick and easy to do and the total can be checked against the till receipt. Mistakes can occur.

When shopping always check sell-by dates. You don't want to have to throw away food which you purchased cheaply but were unable to use in time.

There will be well-known brands of almost everything facing you and advertising can have a very strong sub-conscious pull on you. Apparently it has been calculated that most shoppers take under three seconds to select the brand they want. It is sensible to take a few seconds longer to see if there is a cheaper alternative. One piece of good advice is to keep looking downwards. Many items at eye level on supermarket shelves will be well-known brands which are attractively packaged and which will automatically tempt you to put them in your trolley. Many supermarket 'own brands' are more simply packaged and considerably less expensive. It is always worth experimenting with these. In many cases they will taste just as good and be just as nutritious as the more expensive brand names on the shelves above. Try as many as you can and stick with those you enjoy.

BOX 6 FIVE CHEAP PULSE DISHES

Tuna and bean salad Drain two cans of cannellini beans and toss with flaked tuna, sliced onions, French dressing and parsley.

Boston baked beans Simmer a can of kidney beans, Worcestershire sauce, ketchup, spicy sausage, sliced onion and brown sugar.

Black-eye bean lasagne Mix two cans of drained black-eye beans, a jar of tomato pasta sauce, then layer with sheets of lasagne. Top with cheese sauce and grated cheese and bake until golden.

Chickpea curry Mix two cans of drained chickpeas with a small can of curry sauce; simmer with a small can of chopped tomatoes until thick. Stir in natural yoghurt and serve.

Stuffed peppers Halve, core and de-seed two red peppers. Spoon a can of bean salad into the peppers and top with cheese. Cover with foil, bake until tender, then grill.

NON-SUPERMARKET PURCHASES

Although it is certainly convenient to shop in a supermarket, all shopping doesn't have to be done there. For example, for bulk non-food items consider using a cash and carry store which will normally work out quite a bit cheaper. Although many of these operate primarily as wholesale outlets it is usually possible for the general public to use them.

Non-grocery items usually have a high mark-up in supermarkets, where people buy them purely for the convenience factor, so look elsewhere for them.

Fresh fruit and vegetables can also be bought more cheaply at your local market or greengrocer. Remember that fruit and vegetables that need washing and cutting will invariably be much cheaper than ready-prepared items.

If possible, try to make friends with your local butcher. If you become a regular customer he should be able to provide you with cheap cuts and could even help you plan your menu.

BOX 7 FIVE WAYS TO USE UP LEFT-OVERS

Even the best planned meals often result in left-overs but these can be put to good use.

- Freeze wine in ice-cube trays and use to add to casseroles and sauces.
- Gravy can also be frozen and used in this way.
- Bubble and squeak. Cut left-over vegetables into bite-size pieces and combine with mashed potato and a little gravy. Shallow fry in a little vegetable oil until golden and crispy.
- Don't throw away dry bread. This can be made into crumbs and frozen. These can then be used straight from the freezer.
- Left-over bacon can be tossed with lettuce, tomatoes and French dressing for a quick and easy lunch.

It is also a good idea to do comparison shopping. No doubt you will already have decided to shop in the stores that have the cheapest overall prices and still fulfil the requirements of your weekly shop. 'Free' stamps and loyalty discounts matter little if at the end of the day shopping is still more expensive at those stores that offer them. Even assuming you have found the supermarket in your area that you feel offers the best value, it is still a good idea to make sporadic (perhaps half-yearly) visits to other supermarkets to ensure that this is still the case. Make a list of the essential items on your weekly menu and see how they compare by 'window shopping'. Take a calculator, add up the cost of these essential items and you will soon have a shopping basket league table of supermarkets. Do not be surprised if things have changed and your supermarket is no longer the cheapest in the area. Intense local competition between the various supermarket chains, especially if a new one has opened in the area, can lead to the picture changing very quickly.

By following many of the examples given in this chapter you should be able to make substantial savings in your food budget and these can be put to other areas of your household spending where it is harder to find areas to cut back. A few final tips:

OTHER WAYS TO SAVE MONEY IN THE KITCHEN

- Add breadcrumbs whenever you cook mince.
- Re-use tin foil after carefully washing and smoothing it.
- When roasting meat place it on a meat rack in a baking tray rather than on the bottom of the tin. This saves at least one portion of meat by stopping it sticking.
- Cook dumplings with stew and Yorkshire puddings with a joint!
- Keep biscuit crumbs for pudding bases.
- Cold meat will go much further in sandwiches if it is minced first.

14

AND WHAT ABOUT . . . ?

WORK

The whole area of work is a minefield when it comes to
looking at family priorities. In some families there will be
just one breadwinner; in others both partners will work. In
some cases there will be steady hours but in others there will
be long hours. These too are becoming increasingly flexible
and there is significant pressure to conform to this. With
there being very few jobs for life, difficult choices are often
having to be made. Just how do you get the balance right
between family and work? After all, there is little point
spending so much time providing for your family that there
is no time to spend with them.

For many, particularly men, success is seen as being
something at work: having a prestigious position and the
trappings – big house, expensive cars, etc. – that go with it.
Attempts to achieve this on too fast a time frame can often
lead to resentment at home. This can sadly cause a 'snow-
ball' effect to take place with the man spending more and
more time at work and then being criticised for not caring
for his family. Often the breadwinner thinks he is caring by
providing, whereas the other partner will feel resentful that
they have to do all the inglorious and unpaid work at home
for no financial reward and precious little thanks. Balance is
vital. It is unlikely that on our death beds we will say, 'I wish
I had spent more time at the office'! So value any partner
who is at home. They are not 'only' or 'just' a housewife.

Resolving this sort of situation obviously depends on the individual circumstances of each family but I would suggest that it is both thought about and talked about on the following lines:

- Discuss and agree your priorities. Basic income generation is largely a function of the particular vocation you are in. If significant extra money can be earned by doing overtime or working unsociable hours you need to agree between you just how much more you should work. This is also true if you are self-employed or work from home.

- Many men have an in-built drive to provide for their family both in terms of things and in terms of security. If a man is encouraged and thanked by his non-working partner he will feel that his wife is content with his income and will thus be far less inclined to overwork.

- Where both partners are working, again there needs to be mutual agreement about this. For example, I have spoken to many men who feel failures because their wives 'have' to go out to work even though it means leaving very young children with babyminders. Please do not misunderstand me. I am *not* saying that wives or mothers shouldn't work or even that they can't be the breadwinner in the family. I am saying that this does have to be worked out openly and honestly between you.

- Try to both be flexible. If one partner constantly criticises the other because they 'need' new carpets, windows, etc., they cannot then complain if the partner is never around because they are always working. They think they are doing it to get the very things that will make the other happy! Similarly there

may be occasions when work demands extra hours –
particularly if you're working in a seasonal industry,
for example.

● Remember, you are not indispensable to your workplace but you are to your family! Your children need
you now, not next year, and they need you spending
quality time with them.

REDUNDANCY

One of the main pressures for working long hours is the fear
of redundancy if you fail to be compliant at work. But
working longer hours is by no means an insurance against
redundancy. It can strike anyone, and as society changes
ever more quickly this trend is only going to accelerate.
Many people will therefore have to learn two or more jobs
in their lifetime and most people can expect to face redundancy at least once while working. If you or your
partner do lose your job there is a range of things you
should do:

● Examine your situation at work. Do you have a
contract of employment? If so, look at the length of
notice you must be given. Sometimes you could be
paid in lieu of notice and asked to leave straight away.
If you are near retirement age you might want to ask
for early retirement instead. This can be a good option
if you think you will struggle to get another job, as you
may well be able to draw pension benefits early.

● In some circumstances it may be possible to negotiate
with your employers. You might persuade them to let
you keep your company car if it is in your family
interests to do so. They may be prepared to keep you
in the company pension scheme for a limited time
while you try and find another job.

- Check your contract to ensure that you have got at least the minimum statutory requirement. You will have had to have been in the job for at least two years to qualify. Your payment is then based on the length of service with your employer, although other factors, such as age and a maximum weekly wage figure, complicate the scene.

- Many employers have schemes which offer more than the statutory minimum. Your contract should show you whether you are entitled to anything more.

- Redundancy payments are tax-free up to a generous level. If you are given more than this you will normally have to pay tax on it although if it is in your family's interest you can always use the excess by putting it into your pension plan.

- Explore the benefit system. (This will be looked at briefly later in the chapter.) Many people who have got jobs straight from school or university will have had no experience of how the benefit system works. When you leave work you should be given a P45 form with your final payslip. It is important that you sign on at the local unemployment benefit office as soon as you leave your job. This is not only to ensure that you get the Jobseeker's Allowance as soon as possible but also because your National Insurance contribution will be paid for you once you sign on. Depending on your assets situation, you may well be entitled to other benefits as well. Seek advice.

- Look at your budget. Now that your job has been lost and income is going to be lower, are there areas you can really cut back on? Are there creditors you need to write to, such as your building society, in the hope that they may be able to temporarily help you? Bear in mind that your fuel and lighting bills can soar if you lose your job and stay at home when the house would otherwise usually be empty.

- Check whether you have redundancy insurance. This can protect not only your mortgage payments but often other goods you are purchasing on credit as well.

- Take your time to weigh up the options as to what is best for your family. Do not be rushed into investing a lump sum payment, for example. You should not tie up any of your money for a long period of time until you are certain that you will not need it immediately. It is a good idea to take solid independent advice in all areas of insurance, pensions and investments.

- Plan looking for another job. Discuss with your partner the best options for the family. This could be the chance to change career, move to another part of the country or even for your partner to become the breadwinner! Leave nothing out of the discussions. Your skills, qualifications, experiences, age, locations and job security are all important factors to discuss, as well as the circumstances of your own individual family.

- Don't be afraid to spend money to help you get the right job. Paying for a professionally prepared CV, for example, could repay the cost many times over.

- Spend your time fruitfully. Try and maintain discipline. Visit job clubs. Go to the library and read the newspapers there. This will not only widen the range of jobs available to you but could also save you money if you would otherwise be at home alone using light and heating.

- Think carefully before deciding to work for yourself. A considerable number of people, particularly if they have received a bundle of rejection letters, think about setting up business on their own. If you do consider this, especially when using lump sum redundancy money to do so, make sure you check things carefully and do not rush in. Do you have the right qualifications? Is there the demand? Do you have the appropriate property, insurance, etc.? Are there any grants available? Do you have enough capital? Are you pricing things correctly? Do you understand the need to have a steady cash flow? You can be the best electrician in the world but without appropriate business skills you will probably not survive financially. Remember, even allowing for the capital outlay, it will probably be some time before you come into profit. So seek advice. Your local Jobcentre, Training and Enterprise Council and bank will all be able to help.

- Whatever you do, do not switch yourself off. I know what it is like to be made redundant and the fear and pain that it can bring. However, it is important to realise that you have not been written off for ever just because you have been made redundant. It may turn out to be the start of an exciting new chapter in your life and one which has your family at its centre.

TIME MANAGEMENT

In the hectic world in which we live time management is one of the hardest things to get right. Striking a balance between work and leisure, family time and personal pursuits seems increasingly difficult, particularly when taking into account the demands of young children. It is important to remember that however hard you're working for your family's future, your partner and your children need you now.

If possible, try to allocate a certain amount of time each

month both for family events and also for being with just
your partner or one of your children. Plan to do things that
will be enjoyable to both. Often this can cost little or
nothing – a family walk, visits to the library, watching
local sports events, etc. – but on occasions you will need to
spend money that has been specially set aside for the
purpose. Even if money gets tight try not to let this slip.
It is so easy for children to think that work comes first.
Remember, too, that children's love cannot be bought.
They would much rather be with you than merely have
expensive things that you have given them.

BENEFITS

The whole subject of benefits tends to fill many people with
horror. On the one hand you may read of benefit 'hot-lines'
where people can ring in and report people who are abusing
the system by claiming things to which they are not entitled.
On the other hand there are literally billions of pounds not
claimed every year that rightfully could be. The object lesson
really would appear to be: if in doubt, claim. It is also worth
remembering that benefits change as do the figures where the
cut-off starts. So, for example, just because you were refused
Family Credit several years ago this does not mean that you
will never be entitled to it. If your family has a child with
health problems that lead to him or her needing significant
attention, or an aged relative living with you, there will be
allowances you can claim. Some are dependent on the
amount of available resources you are entitled to claim.
You should first get a copy of the leaflet 'Which Benefit?'
(FB2) and if after reading that you are still uncertain, contact
your local Benefits Agency.

Some of the main benefits include:

Jobseeker's Allowance
This replaced Unemployment Benefit in October 1996.
Providing enough National Insurance has been paid,

anyone who was working is entitled to this although it is now paid for only six months rather than the previous twelve. This in effect means that it very much depends on the amount of capital you have whether your family will continue to get state support if you still do not have a job after six months.

Incapacity Benefit

This has replaced the earlier Sickness Benefit. The main difference is that for new claims after April 1995 payments are taxable after twenty-eight weeks.

Income Support

This is the main benefit for people with low incomes who are not in full-time work. Income Support is a very important benefit because once it has been agreed that you are entitled to it you can also qualify for other benefits such as free prescriptions and school meals, council tax benefits and help with rent or mortgage interest costs. To claim it, both your income and capital have to be below a certain level, you must not be in full-time work or education and you must be actively seeking employment unless specifically exempted from doing so. You need to claim for all the members of your family for whom you are responsible.

Family Credit

Family Credit is in effect a tax-free benefit for low-paid workers with children, and counts as a 'top-up' to your wages when you work more than a certain number of hours each week. This is one of the benefits that is significantly under-claimed. Qualification depends on all your circumstances including, for example, the number of children you have. So if you have applied before and been turned down do not let this put you off applying again – particularly if your income has dipped or you have added to your family since then. Once Family Credit is granted it is paid to you regardless of any changes in circumstances for the next twenty-six weeks.

Housing Benefit

This is paid to people who have a low income and who rent their homes. It can be paid regardless of whether you are in full-time work and can be paid in addition to either Income Support or Family Credit.

In addition to the above there is a whole range of benefits that could apply to your family. Some, such as student grants and Child Benefit, are commonplace. But you may also possibly be entitled to some of the following – Childcare Allowance, Maternity Allowance, social fund maternity payments, school uniform grants, Attendance and Invalidity Allowance, etc., etc. The list is very long.

If you are struggling financially and you think it possible that you might be entitled to some benefits, talk to your local Benefits Agency or Citizens' Advice Bureau.

ADVICE

If you have managed to get this far in the book you will have realised by now that money is a complex and complicated subject! Nearly all of us will have learnt little about it and so will frequently be coming across new situations where we have no experience or expertise; often, nothing is remembered from school or college to give us any idea what to do. So advice is vital. But where do we turn? At this stage the best advice I can give you is to seek the most professional advice you can find in the area that you specifically need it, and always ask yourself one question: Does the person who is giving me this advice stand to benefit financially if I go along with it?

There may, of course, be occasions when you consider that this is not a problem. For example, a professionally prepared CV could make an awful lot of sense to you. But in general you need to be wary about paying for financial advice. The Birmingham Settlement, the Consumer Credit Counselling Service, money advice centres and Credit Action all provide counselling and materials free of charge to anyone facing debt problems. Equally, any benefit problems should be sorted out by a Citizens' Advice Bureau or the Benefits Agency themselves. Seeking advice about savings and pensions is obviously more difficult. Seek recommendations from people you respect and then ask two basic questions. First, is the adviser able to give you advice about all the available products or is he 'tied' to any particular financial institution which may or may not have the right product for you? And second, try and determine that the product being recommended to you really is the one that gives the greatest benefit to you rather than the highest commission to him! A list of the addresses that may help you are at the end of this book.

15

CONCLUSION

Money is not an end in itself. Yes, your family undoubtedly needs it and handling it involves both hard work and sensible management. But if it means working extraordinarily long hours to the detriment of your family it may well be that somewhere along the line priorities have got muddled. Striving for or over-committing yourself for something in the short term in a desperate attempt to keep up with the Joneses can even lead to the disintegration of the family. So although we live in a consumerist society where we want instant gratification, try and plan your money management over the longer term. Set goals and priorities and then make sure that your spending, saving and giving match them.

It is also important to keep using your head! Just a little bit of thought about the needs of your family and how best they can be met may not just save a fair degree of money but sometimes free up valuable time as well. So if you need regular prescriptions have you considered buying pre-payment certificates? Do you think it would be sensible to use savings stamps for fuel, telephone and TV licence? How about hiring a video camera for that holiday or party rather than buying one and leaving it in the box for years? Is your daughter ringing her boyfriend at the cheapest time possible – and are you monitoring the length (if not the content!) of those calls? Are you buying books you won't need again that you could just get out of the library for free? Are you taking advantage of discounts, Air Miles, stamps, etc.? The list is endless. Handling money can be fun for all the family.

Plan for the long term, work hard but spend lots of time with them and you will strike a healthy balance. By being responsible in handling your money in this way all members of your family will learn financial maturity and be truly appreciative of all you do for them.

ADDRESS LIST

Association of British Credit Unions
Unit 307
Westminster Business Square
33 Kennington Lane
LONDON
SE11 5QY

Birmingham Settlement
318 Summer Lane
BIRMINGHAM
B19 3RL

Care for the Family
136 Newport Road
CARDIFF
CF2 1DJ

Consumer Credit Counselling Service
Wade House
Merrion Centre
LEEDS
LS2 8NG

Credit Action
6 Regent Terrace
CAMBRIDGE
CB2 1AA

Independent Financial Advisers
17–19 Emery Road
Brislington
BRISTOL
BS4 5PG

National Savings
FREEPOST BJ2092
BLACKPOOL
FY3 9XR

Pickerings
48 South Street
ALDERLEY EDGE
Cheshire
SK9 7ES